W9-AYE-138

The Book of Miracles

The Book of Miracles

Extraordinary Events in Ordinary Lives

———✳———

Malcolm Day

A QUARTO BOOK

Copyright © 2002 Quarto Inc.

First edition for the United States, its territories
and dependencies and Canada published in 2002
by Barron's Educational Series, Inc.

All rights reserved. No part of this book may be
reproduced in any form, by photostat, microfilm,
xerography, or any other means, or incorporated
into any information retrieval system, electronic
or mechanical, without the written permission of
the copyright owner.

All inquiries should be addressed to:
Barron's Educational Series, Inc.
250 Wireless Boulevard
Hauppauge, New York 11788
http://www.barronseduc.com

ISBN 0-7641-5458-3

Library of Congress Catalog
Card No. 2001093896

QUAR.MIRC

Conceived, designed, and produced by
Quarto Publishing plc
The Old Brewery
6 Blundell Street
London N7 9BH

Project Editor Tracie Lee Davis
Art Editor Karla Jennings
Assistant Art Director Penny Cobb
Designer Caroline Grimshaw
Editor Gillian Kemp
Photographer Michael Wicks/Will White
Illustrator Martin Sanders
Picture Research Image Select International
Proofreader Anne Plume
Indexer Dorothy Frame

Art Director Moira Clinch
Publisher Piers Spence

Manufactured by Universal Graphics
Pte Ltd ., Singapore
Printed by Midas
Printing Ltd., China

9 8 7 6 5 4 3 2 1

Contents

MIRACLES OF JESUS

MIRACLES OF THE CHRISTIAN ERA

Introduction

A miracle is defined for the purposes of this book as a wondrous phenomenon, beyond the laws of nature and within the grasp of our senses. Whether one believes in them or not, miracles have always exerted a fascination on even the most stubborn of minds. The reader is invited to make up his or her own mind on 50 of the most impressive of Christian miracles. They are reported with evidence for and against, including eyewitness accounts and the results of scientific analysis.

The book is divided into two parts, the first outlining the best-known miracles of Jesus, the second presenting the most impressive of miraculous events since the resurrection of Christ. Although Jesus' miracles are unique in the history of the world of faith, he set the mold for living a life so dedicated to God that, as he said, "He who believes in me will also do the works that I do."(John 14:12). It is interesting to see how in Part Two events believed to be miraculous often involve themes, such as protection and cure, that relate to the miracles of Jesus.

Within each of the two parts, chapters carry particular themes. The selected miracles are sequenced chronologically. Perhaps most intriguing of all is the gathering momentum of divine intervention perceived toward the end of the millennium. A micropedia section at the end of the book documents some of the amazing things that have happened in recent years.

Part One

Miracles of Jesus

Modern responses to the miracles of Jesus are remarkably varied. They range from a literal acceptance of the events described in the Gospels, to the rejection of anything contrary to the laws of nature as purely mythological expression.

The mere fact that Gospel narratives of the same event differ in their details gives ammunition to the skeptic who will claim that the sources are unreliable. Some scholars say that the same event acquired a greater sense of the miraculous at each telling (the Gospels range in date from about 65 to 95 C.E.), and that originally the events described may have been merely parable stories.

But the modern mind is very different from that of 1st-century Palestine, when Jesus lived. There was then little scientific knowledge—the people believed the world to be small and flat, and there were no known "laws of nature" such as we understand today. In that day, all existed within the realm of God, and all was the responsibility of God. As Jesus said—Not one sparrow shall fall to the ground without the will of the Father. In narrating the miracles, the Gospel writers expected their readers to marvel at the stories they would readily believe to be manifestations of the glory of God at work in this world. As such, the miracles were extensions of what God was controlling day in, day out. Far from being an obstruction to faith, as they are to the modern mind, the miracles enhanced faith.

Nature Miracles

It was taken for granted in Palestine at the time of Jesus of Nazareth that nothing happened without God or the devil having a hand in it. But when an individual comes along and demonstrates his power over nature, it is seen to be a supreme act of God with a special purpose.

Creation was commonly believed to have involved God in a desperate but finally victorious contest with the forces of chaos and evil, yet dark forces still lurked in the world. When Jesus calms the storm, he is said to "rebuke" the wind, as though speaking to someone, a demonic spirit. Jesus exorcised the wind and the waves as if they were possessed people. Fortunes, good and ill, were all considered to be the result of moral behavior—a bountiful harvest was reward for good; a blight, pestilence, or disaster were all too readily seen as punishments for sin. In the Old Testament the ten plagues sent to the Egyptian Pharaoh, when Moses was endeavoring to release the Israelites from captivity, were seen as miracles of divine retribution on the wicked Pharaoh. The ensuing parting of the "Sea of Reeds" that allowed their escape was a miraculous affirmation that God would save his people Israel. Thereafter any miracle over nature was seen as a sign that God's plan of salvation for mankind was on track, though the manifestations nearly always carried the rider that man must have faith if he or she is to be saved.

By the time of Jesus, salvation had largely evolved from being a collective prize for the nation to an individual pursuit. The nature miracles appealed to the individual to believe, not because of the wondrous effects he or she might see but because of their significance. All of the nature miracles carried essential teaching about the nature of God. They were performed in the presence of the disciples because, of all the people who witnessed Jesus, it was they who were closest to him. Jesus therefore hoped that they would understand the purpose of these miracles. Often their response was one of fear and panic, and therefore fell short of Jesus' ideal of complete trust in God.

Sea of Galilee

Bethlehem *Dead Sea*

[Matthew 1:18–2:2]

The Virgin Birth

O ne of the most controversial miracles associated with Christ is that he was born of a virgin. New Testament references to it are restricted to the two Christmas accounts in the Gospels of St. Matthew and St. Luke.

What the Scholars Say. . .

———※———

In their enthusiasm to find fulfillment of the prophecy of Isaiah chapter 7, the evangelists mistranslated the Hebrew word *ha'almah* as "virgin," when it really means "young woman." The prophecy was uttered when Jerusalem was besieged in the 8th century B.C.E. God sent Isaiah to reassure the Judeans that their city would not fall into enemy hands. Thus, the prophecy was expected to be fulfilled in that time. It is unusual to expect a second fulfillment, 700 years later!

In Nazareth of Galilee, a couple by the names of Mary and Joseph were due to be married. They were serving their one-year betrothal, an obligatory period prior to the wedding, in which they were treated as man and wife but did not yet have the full rights enjoyed in marriage. During this period, it was discovered that Mary was carrying a child in her womb. Joseph, being a man of principle but also wishing to protect her honor, decided to have the marriage contract dissolved secretly. While he was making his plans, an angel appeared to him in a dream saying, "Joseph, do not hesitate to take Mary as your wife; for that which has been conceived within her has come from the Holy Spirit. She will bear a son, and you must call him 'Jesus,' for it is he who will save his people from their sins." The angel continued by saying how this event would fulfill the prophecy of Isaiah that "a virgin will conceive and bear a son."

When Joseph awoke, he did as the angel commanded and accepted Mary as his wife.

Left The birth of Jesus depicted in this 15th-century miniature, was heralded by an angel and a bright star.

What the Astronomers Say. . .

——— ✳ ———

The gospel evidence for the date of Jesus' birth is inconclusive, and it could have happened any time between 6 B.C.E. and 6 C.E. An intriguing constellation occurred just before sunrise on August 12 in 3 B.C.E., when the planet Jupiter rose in conjunction with Venus, the "morning star." A blazing light would have been seen in the sky. As Jupiter is considered astrologically to be the father of the gods and Venus the goddess of fertility, the conjunction of the two planets may have been interpreted as heralding the birth of a king. Furthermore, the orbit of Jupiter across the sky would have paused to change direction on December 25, 2 B.C.E., moving from Jerusalem toward Bethlehem.

He did not have sexual relations with her until her son was born, in Bethlehem. Joseph named the child Jesus. After his birth, astrologers from the east came to pay homage to Jesus, having observed the rising of his star.

Water Into Wine

[John 2:1–11]

The first of the miracles recorded in St. John's Gospel takes place in a little Galilean village called Cana, thought to be the modern Kafar Kanna situated near Nazareth.

Jesus, his mother Mary, and the disciples were attending a wedding when there arose a serious breach of social etiquette – the wine ran out. In a society where hospitality was regarded as a great honor for the host, one can imagine the embarrassment and shame at the prospect of guests sitting with empty cups in their hands on such a big occasion. Mary expressed her concern to Jesus, who in turn made a curious reference to his destiny before proceeding to act in the crisis.

He pointed out six large jars used for ritual washing and ordered the servants to fill them with water. The servants then drew more water from the well and handed it to the steward of the feast who, upon tasting it, hailed the bridegroom saying, "Everyone serves the best wine first, and waits until the guests have drunk freely before serving the poorer sort; but you have kept the best wine till last!"

Thus the steward and most of the guests were unaware of the social calamity that Jesus had just averted by turning the water into wine. Only the servants knew what had happened.

Left More gravity than is customary at a Jewish wedding celebration hangs in the air in this medieval portrayal of the crisis at Cana.

Spiritual Banquet?

It is thought that St. John the evangelist saw in the miracle at Cana a pointer to Jesus' mission on earth. The number of purification jars was six, one short of the number representing completion in Judaism. It is as though the evangelist is signifying that only through the coming of Christ would Judaism be fulfilled, when the Jewish faith would be infused with the Holy Spirit, as symbolized by the transformation of water into wine. It is possible that John also understood the wedding feast to be analogous to the future church, in which Jesus would be the bridegroom and the church his bride.

Myth of Dionysus

St. John wrote his gospel in Ephesus, a Greek city in Asia Minor, for a Greek readership. He would have been aware of their familiarity with the myth of the god of wine, Dionysus, who also was believed to have made wine from water.

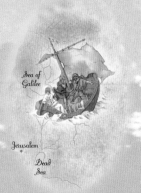

Sea of
Galilee

Jerusalem
*
Dead
Sea

[Mark 4:35–41]

The Calming
of the Storm

I n antiquity, one of the sure signs of being in possession of divine power was the ability to control the elements, which were thought to issue directly from the heavens.

Jesus had been preaching for most of the day, some of the time while sitting in a fishing boat at the sea shore. In the evening he and his disciples put out in the boat to escape the thronging crowd. As sometimes happened on the Sea of Galilee, a storm blew up suddenly. Wind and waves lashed the boat, which filled fast with water. The disciples grew more and more agitated, especially as their master appeared to be unperturbed, being asleep on a cushion in the stern.

"Master, do you not care that we are sinking?" they cried in despair. Jesus woke and spoke to the sea, "Peace, be still," whereupon the storm subsided. Once again there was calm. Jesus asked them why they were so afraid, "Do you still have no faith?" The disciples were awestruck and wondered who was this, that even the forces of nature obeyed.

What the Skeptics Say . . .
———※———

This inland sea is located in part of the Jordan rift valley, and lies 220 yards (200 m) below sea level. Mountains and gorges to the west act as funnels when a west wind blows, causing it to rush onto the lake with great ferocity. The skeptics say that the storm may have died away as quickly as it arose, and that therefore what the church later recorded as a miracle of Jesus in fact had its origin in a naturally occurring event.

Right The Sea of Galilee has a unique microclimate prone to suddenly producing extreme weather conditions.

Feeding the Five Thousand

I n the only miracle recorded in all four Gospels, Jesus feeds a huge crowd of hungry followers with five loaves of bread and two fish.

[Mark 6:30–44;
Matthew 14:13–21;
Luke 9:10–17;
John 6:1–13]

The disciples had returned from several days of evangelizing and Jesus took them to a deserted place so they could rest and recover. But as they set sail in a small boat across the Sea of Galilee, the crowd, which had been following them for days, saw where they were heading and went around the lake on foot to where they would land. On coming ashore, Jesus ministered to the multitudes until late in the day. The disciples grew anxious that the people would get hungry, and suggested that Jesus send them off to fetch provisions. They were taken aback when Jesus replied that they themselves should provide the food.

They had no money, and as for food, all that could be found was what a little boy had with him, five loaves and two small fish. Jesus, unperturbed, told the disciples to get the crowd seated. Then came the moment of truth. He blessed the food, broke the loaves, and divided the fish, and gave the food to the disciples to distribute. Everyone ate to their heart's content, and the leftovers filled twelve large baskets.

What the Skeptics Say . . .

———— ✳ ————

It is curious that none of the Gospel writers describe any detail of the miracle. Some scholars think that the people had in fact brought food with them, and it was only Jesus' spirit of generosity that prompted them to share it. This in itself could be seen as a minor miracle, and one consistent with the message of Jesus that we should love our neighbor as we love ourselves.

Above A late medieval French version of the miracle shows
the expectant crowd gathered for the moment of truth.

Sea of
Galilee
Bethsaida

Jerusalem

Dead
Sea

[Matthew 14:22–33]

What the Scholars Say . . .

———✳———

There is some debate about how the Greek, in which the Gospels were written, should be translated. The words that are translated as "on the sea" can also mean "by the sea." If the coastline was indented, Jesus may well have been walking toward them, but still on land. In the partial light of the moon, perhaps with some early morning sea mist, conditions may have produced the effect of Jesus apparently walking on the sea.

Walking on Water

I mmediately following the Feeding of the Five Thousand comes perhaps the most beguiling of Jesus' miracles, when he was seen walking on the Sea of Galilee at night.

Jesus retired to the hills to pray alone while the disciples set off ahead of him by boat to Bethsaida. The sea was rough and they struggled to row against a strong headwind. Their progress was slow. It was between three and six in the morning, when they were some way out to sea, that they beheld the extraordinary sight of a form walking on the sea, coming toward them. The disciples were terrified as they thought it must be a ghost. Then came the utterance, "It is I; have no fear."

Peter called out, asking that if it was indeed their Lord to tell him to walk over to Him. Peter was bidden, so he stepped out of the boat and to his amazement began to walk over the water toward Jesus. But when he felt the strength of the wind again, he became afraid and started to sink. He cried out, "Save me, Lord." Jesus reached out and caught hold of him, saying, "Why did you doubt? How little faith you have." They climbed into the boat and the wind dropped. The other disciples in the boat fell at Jesus' feet, saying, "Truly you are the Son of God."

Sea of
Galilee

Jerusalem

Dead
Sea

[John 21:1–14]

What the Church Says . . .

——— ✳ ———

• The meal on the beach was a reminder of the Last Supper and the glory of the resurrection, and it also recalled the miracle of the feeding of the 5000.

• The number of fish was specified as 153. Scholars say that this number is based on a tradition that there are 153 species of fish in the world, and that the catch represents all the races in the world who would be converted to Christianity. The fact that the net did not break means that no nation would be excluded.

The Great haul of Fish

The third time that Jesus appeared to his disciples after his resurrection from the dead was beside the Sea of Tiberias. It was a mysterious occasion.

He called out to them, asking if they had caught anything. When they replied that they had not, he told them to throw the net to starboard, and they would make a catch. They did so, and found that there were so many fish in their net that they were unable to haul them aboard. Then the disciple whom Jesus loved was convinced of who the figure was and told Peter. When Peter heard this, he plunged into the sea and went to see for himself. The others followed in the boat.

Coming ashore, the disciples saw a charcoal fire with fish laid on it and some bread. The stranger told them to bring some of their catch, which Peter did. They had landed 153 fish in total, and despite the large number, the net had not broken under the strain. The man offered them breakfast. None of the disciples felt bold enough to ask the stranger who he was, yet in their hearts they felt it had to be the risen Christ. He took the bread and gave it to them, and did the same with the fish.

Above Raphael's stylized version of the disciples'
encounter with the risen Christ captures the
magical sense of his manifestation at dawn.

healing Miracles

Greek culture pervaded Palestine in the 1st century C.E. Beliefs in astrology and magic jostled alongside traditional Jewish faith in one God and a coming Messiah who would deliver the Jews out of their enemies' hands.

Scored deep in the national psyche was the idea that their subservience to Gentile (i.e. Roman) rulers was a punishment from God. Around the time of the life of Jesus, there was a sea change in the thinking about redemption. Salvation shifted from being a national concern to an individual one. Some groups, such as the Zealots, still expected the Messiah to deliver the nation, but others saw a need for redemption at a personal level. In turn, this meant renouncing sin. To do so was an act of holistic cleansing – of total mind, body, and spirit. And this was part of Jesus' message. He came as a healer of the whole person. In Palestine, illness and disease were very much linked to the well-being of the spirit and mind.

Medication and surgery were available for wealthier Roman citizens, but hardly touched the fringe of 1st-century Palestine. There were no public health institutions, and doctors were unaffordable (St. Mark's Gospel records one woman spending all the money she had on treatments that failed). Generally, it was the rabbis who made pronouncements on medical conditions. Apothecaries

would prepare oils, ointments, and potions
for the sick. Apart from ministering to minor
injuries and ailments, medicine was of limited use.
The wise ones knew of the importance of the spirit in
healing: "A cheerful heart is good medicine, but a
crushed spirit dries up the bones." (Proverbs 17:22)

Many of the physically and mentally ill were driven from
their communities to live as beggars. Lepers and demoniacs had
to dwell on the edge of towns. Sanitation was poor, and Jews were
punctilious about washing hands before eating meals. Homes were
usually crowded, with people sharing space with animals. The lack of
hygiene meant that infection and disease spread easily and life expectancy
was short. It is no wonder that someone with the healing power Jesus
possessed should attract so much attention.

[Mark 1:21–28]

Exorcism at Capernaum

The first of Jesus' miracles happened at a synagogue in Capernaum, a village on the shore of the Sea of Galilee. The gathered people were almost spellbound by his teaching, the power of which had not been experienced before.

What the Scholars Say . . .

———✳———

Exorcism was widely regarded in the ancient world as an instrument of magic. Invisible powers were believed to operate in the universe, and it was thought that secret knowledge could unlock and destroy their potency. The ability to perform an exorcism, however, was not in itself proof of divine authority. Indeed, the witnesses' reactions in this episode suggest that they were more impressed by the power in Jesus' teaching than by the casting out of demons.

Unlike the scribes who normally taught at the synagogue, Jesus seemed to teach with an extraordinary authority, as though his words were divinely inspired. The aura was such that a man present suddenly yelled out, "What do you want with us, Jesus of Nazareth? Have you come to destroy us? I know who you are – the Holy One of God!"

At this, Jesus reprimanded the man, saying, "Be silent, and come out of him." The man, who was possessed by an evil spirit, was apparently thrown to the floor by an inner force and sent into convulsions. With a loud cry, the spirit suddenly left him. All present were at first speechless, then in astonishment they began to talk about this new kind of teaching, how even evil spirits obeyed it. The news about Jesus spread rapidly, and he was soon spoken about all over the district.

Right Jesus healing the possessed man in a 17th-century engraving by Matthaus Merlan from the Merian Bible.

What the Skeptics Say . . .

———— ✳ ————

The man who was considered to be possessed might today, with the benefit of medical knowledge, have been diagnosed as an hysteric or epileptic. The highly charged atmosphere of the occasion inside Capernaum's tiny synagogue may well have generated enough stress in the subject to trigger a fit. Later on in St. Mark's Gospel, there is such a case of an epileptic boy being cured.

The Paralyzed Man

[Mark 2:1–12]

Fame came fast to Jesus. It was not long before he could not go anywhere without a big crowd following him.

Many people gathered at his house, both inside and out, in order to hear him preach. Four men who brought a paralyzed man to be healed could not get him near Jesus. They climbed the outside staircase to the roof, unpacked the rafters, and lowered the man on his stretcher to where Jesus was sitting. When Jesus saw the strength of their belief, he said to the paralyzed man, "My son, your sins are forgiven."

Jesus said this partly to test some experts in the Hebrew law who were sitting with him, knowing that they would think it blasphemous to claim to be able to forgive sins. To them, Jesus said, "Is it easier to say to a paralyzed man 'Your sins are forgiven' or to say 'Stand up, take your bed and walk'?" He continued by saying that authority to forgive sins had been granted to him. To emphasize the point, he told the paralytic to pick up his stretcher and walk—which he did, to everyone's amazement. The crowd parted incredulously to allow the healed man to pass.

What the Scholars Say . . .

———— ✳ ————

It was believed in Palestine that illness was the consequence of sin. So, by implication, if Jesus could forgive sin, the cause of the disease would be removed and the symptoms would disappear. By pronouncing the paralyzed man forgiven, Jesus had effected the cure. The authorities were suspicious of healers whom they accused of being magicians performing without divine authority. What set Jesus apart from the rest was that his power was perceived to emanate from God.

Right Jesus healing the sick in a 17th-century engraving by Matthaus Merian from the Merian Bible.

Sea of Galilee
Capernaum
Cana
Jerusalem
Dead Sea

The Courtier's Son

When Jesus returned to Cana, the village where he had turned water into wine, he met a royal courtier whose son was seriously ill in Capernaum.

[John 4:46–54]

Distance Healing

——— ✳ ———

Certain healers claim to be endowed with a spiritual power that will effect cures through touch and across great distances. This facility is said to have been possessed by Jesus of Nazareth, Krishna, and the Buddha. Since energy travels at the speed of light, there is no limitation of time or distance on its transmission. The brain of the recipient is said to receive signals like a television. Having the will to recover is said to be important as it facilitates the flow of energy in the path of least resistance.

The courtier of Herod's palace begged Jesus to go down to Capernaum and cure his son who was close to death. Jesus said to the people gathered around him, "Will none of you ever believe without seeing signs and sensational works?" The courtier again pleaded with Jesus for help before his son died. Jesus assured him that he could go home, and that his son would live.

The man believed what Jesus said and started out on his journey home, some 20 miles away. While still some way off, he met his servants coming the other way. They said that his boy was recovering, that he was going to live. Trembling with joy, the courtier asked them when his son had begun to recover, and they replied that the fever left him the day before, at one o'clock in the afternoon. The father noted that this was exactly the time when he was with Jesus.

What the Scientists Say . . .

———✳———

Research reveals that the work of healers can produce remarkable results. Recipients may experience spontaneous biochemical reactions, such as a rise in the level of the adrenal hormone DHEA that is central to the protection of the body against illnesses, including heart disease, cancer, arthritis, and diabetes. Cells associated with the body's immune system are activated and increased by the healing process.

Demons Into Swine

When Jesus and his disciples came to the eastern side of the Sea of Galilee, to the Gentile district of the Gerasenes, Jesus was confronted by a madman as soon as he stepped ashore.

[Mark 5:1–20]

What the Scholars Say . . .

——— ✳ ———

The ancient world was obsessed with the idea of demons who were thought to be as plentiful then as viruses are today. People who were sick were especially vulnerable. If they started to believe that they were possessed by a demon, it was possible that symptoms might develop psychosomatically. Such was the magnitude of this demoniac's possession that he identified himself by the name of Legion, a Roman regiment normally 6000 strong.

The man lived among the tombs where he howled day and night. The people of the nearby town had tried to tie him up but even chains were useless. He broke free and ran wild, often gashing his limbs on stones. When he saw Jesus in the distance, he ran toward him and flung himself at his feet, shouting, "What do you want with me, Jesus, son of the Most High God? In God's name do not torment me." At the same time, Jesus was commanding the spirit in him to come out. He asked him his name and the man replied, "Legion—there are so many of us." He begged Jesus not to send them away.

There happened to be a large herd of pigs feeding on the hillside. The spirits in the man asked if Jesus would send them into the pigs instead. He granted their request, and the spirits infested the herd of some 2000 head, sending them in a crazed rush down the hill and over the cliff into the sea below.

The swineherds ran off and told the townsfolk what had happened. When the people came and saw the former madman sitting in his right mind, they became afraid and told Jesus to leave the area.

Mad Pigs?

——— ✳ ———

It seems unlikely that Jesus deliberately sacrificed a large herd of pigs without considering the financial loss to the owner. One explanation is that the high-pitched shrieking of the madman threw the herd into panic, and bystanders thought the pigs had become possessed. Another explanation is symbolic. There was an expectation that the coming Messiah would destroy the enemies of the Jews. So the demonic Legion, representing the occupying power of Rome in Palestine, were transferred appropriately into Gentile pigs and sent to their deaths.

Left Jesus casts devils out of a kneeling man, and casts them in the Gadarene swine who plunge over the cliff as if possessed. From J. J. Tissot, "Life of our Saviour Jesus Christ," c.1890.

The Sick Man at Bethesda

[John 5:1–15]

While visiting Jerusalem for one of the festivals, Jesus went to the sheep pool of Bethesda where the sick would gather in the hope of receiving a cure.

What Some Scholars Say . . .

——— ✳ ———

The account of this miracle by St. John is an allegory. Accordingly, the pool's five colonnades represent the five "pillars," or books, of the Jewish Law. Just as the colonnades provide shelter but do not heal, so the Law provides a framework for daily life but no means for spiritual growth. The 38 years of the man's illness corresponds to the time mentioned in Deuteronomy that the Israelites spent wandering in the desert before they reached the Promised Land.

It was believed that an angel would at certain times come down to the pool and disturb the surface of the water. The first person to enter it would be cured of his or her illness. Lying about the five colonnades that were features of Bethesda were the blind, the lame, and the paralyzed. Among them was a man who had been crippled for 38 years. Jesus asked him if he really did want to recover. The cripple said he had no one to help him into the pool when the water was disturbed, and that someone always beat him to it. Jesus answered, "Rise to your feet, take up your bed, and walk." Instantly, the man recovered and was able to walk.

Some Jews who were there asked who this man was, but the cured cripple did not know, for Jesus had melted away into the crowd. A little later, Jesus found him again and told him to leave behind his sinful ways in case an even worse misfortune should befall him.

Holy Water

———— ✳ ————

It was believed in the ancient world that certain places attracted particular spirits. Hills, trees, and pools all had their resident spirits. And water springs especially, being the founts of such a precious commodity in a dry land, were often considered to be sacred.

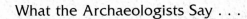

What the Archaeologists Say . . .

———— ✳ ————

Remains within the old walls of Jerusalem show the pool to be deep enough to swim in. There was a subterranean feeder stream, which every now and again would bubble up and disturb the waters. This activity was believed to be caused by an angel.

Above Peter van Lint, (1609-1690), portrays Christ healing the sick man at the Pool of Bethesda, around 1640.

Sea of
Galilee

Jerusalem

Dead
Sea

[John 9:1–41]

Inherited Sin?

———— ✳ ————

The Jews regarded every calamity as a punishment for sin, but when someone was born blind it was harder to account for. The rabbis (Jewish teachers) invented the possibility of prenatal sin to account for inherited defects; hence, the disciples' question of whether the man or his parents were to blame.

The Man Born Blind

During his ministry Jesus healed many who were either deaf, dumb, or blind. While he was in Jerusalem, he encountered a man who had been blind from birth.

Jesus' disciples asked him whether the man was blind because of his own sin or the sin of his parents. Jesus replied that they were missing the point—the man was not born blind as a punishment, but so that God's power might be displayed in curing him. "While I am in the world, I am the light of the world," Jesus said.

With these words he spat on the ground and made a paste with the spittle; he spread it on the man's eyes and said to him, "Go and wash in the pool of Siloam." The man went away and washed, and miraculously when he returned he could see.

The Pharisees (Jewish doctors of the Law) went wild with indignation, interrogating everyone to try to get to the bottom of the healing. An angry debate ensued during which the cured man grew in esteem, while the Pharisees diminished in theirs. At the end Jesus said that he had come into the world to give sight to the sightless, and to make blind those who see. Some Pharisees asked, "Do you mean that we are blind?" He replied, "If you were blind, you would not be guilty, but because you say, 'We see,' your guilt remains."

What Medical Historians Say . . .

———✳———

Eye diseases were quite common in Bible times when general
health and sanitation were poor. Their causes were climatic factors,
infection, venereal disease, heredity, and senility. Venereal infection
can lead to severe conjunctivitis and blindness in newborn infants.
It is possible that the blind man inherited such a condition.

The Ten Lepers

Mediterranean Sea
Sea of Galilee
Jerusalem
Dead Sea

During the last phase of Jesus' life, when he was making his way to Jerusalem, he came upon a band of lepers on the outskirts of a village.

[Luke 17:11–19]

Jesus' fame had spread far and wide, and even these lepers, the outcasts of society, knew of Jesus and recognized him when they saw him coming toward them. Being contagious, the group of them—ten in all—kept their distance and called out to him, asking if he would take pity on them. He told them to go and see the priests, the people who, by law, could pronounce them clean. In great surprise, as they made their way, they realized that they had become clean. One of them, a Samaritan, turned back praising God and fell at Jesus' feet in gratitude for the cure he had effected.

Jesus asked the man why the other nine had not come to thank him too, for had they not also been cured? Only the Samaritan, a foreigner in this land, had come back. And Jesus told him to go, for it was his faith that had cured him.

Right "Christ Healing the Lepers at Capernaum," from J. J. Tissot, "The Life of Our Saviour Jesus Christ," c.1890.

What the Experts Say . . .

———✳———

There were two types of "leprosy" recognized in Palestine. The less serious of the two was not leprosy but a skin condition that could be dermatitis, ringworm, or de-pigmented skin. The second type was real leprosy, caused by bacteria that ate away the flesh. It is not known which disease Jesus confronted in this episode.

Perhaps the worst part of the disease was the psychological trauma that it caused. According to the regulations concerning leprosy written in the Old Testament book of Leviticus, lepers had to cry "Unclean! Unclean!" wherever they went, and had to live in exile. The shame experienced by victims led many to despair and suicide.

The fact that the Jew and Samaritan, by tradition hateful enemies, could in these circumstances forget their differences and be together, indicates the degree of mutual suffering.

Raising the Dead

In Palestine, there were mixed views about what happened when a person died. The Jerusalem high priests, called the Sadducees, had no belief in an afterlife. Life was to be lived in the here and now, and if an individual spent it righteously his or her reward would be enjoyed on earth in the form of a healthy and prosperous old age.

The Pharisees were more progressive thinkers in Jewish society who, as the scribes and rabbis of the synagogues, dealt with the religious lives of the ordinary Jew. They were much more anxious than the Sadducees about what the future held. They believed in a resurrection and a Day of Judgment, when everybody would be reckoned for the way he or she had led his or her life. The good would lead an afterlife in a new golden age on earth, while the bad would suffer eternal punishment. Quite when this day would arrive was a matter for speculation, but many groups thought it was coming soon and that it would be heralded by a Messiah whose mission on earth would be accompanied by such acts as raising the dead, just as the classical prophets

had done in the past. Elijah, for
example, had restored life to a widow's
dead son. Likewise, Jesus raised a
widow's dead son in the town of Nain.

Some believed in apocalyptic visions of the
end of the present era on earth. And there was a hearty
belief in the pursuance of conflict between supernatural forces of good and evil.
Angels and demons were thought to surround human life and would struggle
over an individual's fate. Although people's bodies died and decayed, their souls
were immortal, and when the messianic age dawned, all the righteous souls
would somehow be reunited with their bodily partners in the resurrection.

In anticipation of this return to life, Jews followed certain customs for
burial, which included embalming the dead with spices and incense to ward
off evil spirits. Tombs were artificial caverns hewn from the rock, with carved
benches on which to lay the corpses. The small entrance would be sealed by
rolling a stone across it, to protect the bodies from scavengers. In Jerusalem,
once corpses had completed their decomposition, the bones were often gathered
into an ossuary (wooden box) to save space.

Capernaum
Sea of
Galilee

Jerusalem

Dead
Sea

The Daughter of Jairus

While Jesus was by the shore of the Sea of Galilee, one man among the crowd gathered there was Jairus, leader of one of the synagogues.

[Mark 5:21–43]

What the Scholars Say . . .

————— ✳ —————

Ancient wonder-workers often used formulas in a foreign tongue. It was said that such words lost their power if translated into another language. This may explain why the original Aramaic "*talitha cum*" was retained in this episode (the rest of the Gospel is in Greek). As proof that the miracle has worked the child walks about the room and is also given food to show that she cannot be a ghost, since ghosts do not eat solid food!

When he saw Jesus, Jairus threw himself down at Jesus' feet and begged him to go and lay his hands on his daughter who was at death's door. Although she was now *in extremis* and beyond the help of any earthly power, Jairus believed that it was still possible for Jesus to save her.

However, along the way to Jairus' house, Jesus was held up by an incident in the crowd that was following him, and then a messenger arrived with the news that Jairus' daughter had just died. Jesus told the synagogue leader to have faith. He told the people to leave, all except James, John, and Peter, who accompanied him and Jairus to the house. When they arrived, the usual ritual of mourning was already under way. Jesus went inside and asked why there was so much grief when the girl was not dead but just asleep. He sent away the mourners and allowed only the child's parents and his disciples into the room where the girl lay. Jesus took the girl's hand and said to her, "talitha cum," which means "get up, my child." Immediately, the 12-year-old girl rose from her bed and walked about. Everyone stared at her in amazement, and Jesus told them to feed her.

Below "Christ raising the daughter of Jairus, Governor of the Synagogue, from the dead." Illustrated by J. J. Tissot for his "Life of our Saviour Jesus Christ," 1897.

What the Skeptics Say . . .

————❋————

Some take Jesus' words that the girl was "asleep" literally, and believe she had been wrongly diagnosed as dead. They maintain that she was in a trancelike state, or coma, from which Jesus was able to release her. Certainly those present were in no doubt that she was dead as Jewish mourning was in process. The accounts in Matthew and Luke mention the presence of professional mourners, who would not have been hired at great expense prematurely.

The Raising of Lazarus

Considered by many to be the climax to Jesus' miracles was the restoration to life of a dead man called Lazarus.

[John 11:1–44]

Jerusalem •

Dead
Sea

What the Scholars Say . . .

———— ✻ ————

Unlike the raising of Jairus' daughter, this miracle was performed four days after death. According to Jewish belief, the spirit of a dead man hovers over the body for three days before departing, in the hope of reuniting with it. The first day of decay was the fourth, and henceforth the soul had departed. In stating that Lazarus had been dead four days, St. John made the point that the body was truly dead before it was given life again.

Jesus used to stay with Lazarus when he was visiting Jerusalem at festival times, as Lazarus lived in the village of Bethany just outside the city. When Jesus heard that Lazarus was sick, he did not go immediately to his house, but strangely waited for two days in Galilee. Then, acting upon a moment of intuition, he declared to his disciples that Lazarus had "fallen asleep," which they took literally. But Jesus meant that his friend had died. They then set off on the long walk to Lazarus' house.

On arrival, Jesus discovered that Lazarus had lain dead in a tomb for four days. When his sisters, Mary and Martha, approached Jesus, he told them that their brother would rise again; that if only a person had faith in Jesus, even if that person died, he would come back to life. Martha thought Jesus was referring to the general resurrection, believed to happen at the end of time. When he said mysteriously that he himself was the resurrection, she was puzzled but somehow still believed in him.

Jesus asked to be shown the tomb. It was a cave with a stone placed against it. He asked for the stone to be removed, at which time Martha reminded him that the corpse would

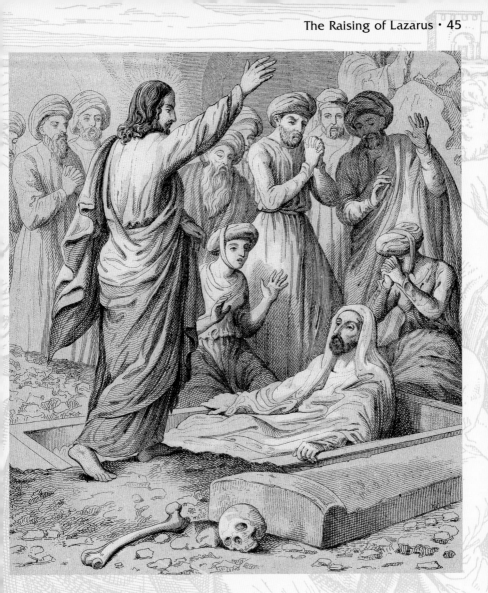

already be smelling from decay. Jesus looked
upward and thanked God aloud for answering his
prayer, and then said, "Lazarus, come out." The
figure of Lazarus slowly emerged from the tomb,
swathed in linen bands from head to foot. Jesus
asked for the man to be unwrapped and let free.

Above An engraving on
wood of the raising of
Lazarus by Jesus, c. 1880.

Sea of
Galilee

Jerusalem
Dead
Sea

[John 20:1–18]

The Resurrection of Jesus

O n the Friday of Jesus' crucifixion two secret disciples, Joseph of Arimathea and Nicodemus, buried the body in a new tomb in a Jerusalem garden. Nicodemus prepared the body according to Jewish burial customs and wrapped it carefully in white linen.

Early on Sunday morning Mary Magdalene came to the tomb. She saw that the stone had been rolled away from the entrance, and ran off to tell Peter and the disciple whom Jesus loved. They both came quickly to the tomb. The beloved disciple peered inside and saw the linen wrappings lying there, but did not go inside. Peter went inside and also saw the napkin that had been placed over Jesus' head.

They went home and left Mary at the tomb. With tears in her eyes, she too peered inside, and to her amazement saw two angels sitting where the body of Christ had been. Something made her turn, and she saw a man standing there. She took him to be the gardener and asked if he had removed the body. Then he said her name, and Mary recognized the man as Jesus. He told her not to touch him, for he would soon ascend to the Father, but to go and tell the others, which she did with great excitement.

A Stolen Body?

—— ✳ ——

If Jesus' enemies had taken the body, they would surely have produced it to prove to his followers that he had not risen from the dead. If his friends had taken it, they would surely not have preached a lie, nor been willing to die for something they manifestly could not have believed in. According to St. Paul, Jesus appeared to more than 500 people in his resurrected state.

What the Church Says . . .

——— ✳ ———

The testimony of a Roman centurion and the piercing of Jesus' side by a spear emphasize that Christ did die on the cross. The new conviction with which his followers boldly confronted those who had condemned Jesus is the strongest evidence for the resurrection, in as much as they were imbued with the power of the Holy Spirit, which Jesus had foretold they would receive.

Below "The Morning of the Resurrection," (1882) by Edward Coley Jones shows the angelic messengers on either side of Mary who is startled by Jesus' appearance.

What the Skeptics Say . . .

——— ✳ ———

According to Mark's Gospel, Pontius Pilate was surprised to hear that Jesus had died so quickly when Joseph of Arimathea asked for permission to bury him. Victims of crucifixion sometimes lingered for days. Some skeptics have suggested that Jesus was not really dead when he was taken down from the cross, and that with the help of Joseph and Nicodemus he escaped.

Part Two

Miracles

of the

"Faith will bring with it these miracles: believers will cast out devils in my name and speak in strange tongues; if they handle snakes or drink any deadly poison, they will come to no harm; and the sick on whom they lay their hands will recover."
(Mark 16:17–18)

. . . So ran Jesus' departing address to his Apostles. And once he had ascended to heaven, the Acts of the Apostles records the descent of the Holy Spirit in the form of tongues of fire. That was the Day of Pentecost, which heralded not only a period when the Apostles would be empowered to carry out the sort of works Jesus had done, but a whole era of Christianity in which the Holy Spirit would act as intermediary for Christ on earth.

What has happened since the resurrection of Christ is believed to be a series of revelations of the divine through humanity. Some believe that, for instance, the Apparitions of Mary—so numerous in the 20th century—together weave a beautiful connected mosaic of heaven showing the presence of God in the world. Most miracles recorded here involve manifestations of Christ and his mother Mary. In some cases the two appear together.

As the only official judge for Roman Catholics of whether an occurrence is to be accepted as an authentic supernatural intervention—and even then, to be sure that it is divine and not diabolic in origin—the Roman Catholic church is

Christian Era

extremely cautious in its process of approval. The Vatican is as skeptical as anyone in its consideration of the large number of miracle claims presented to it. A painstaking investigation can take decades, and will involve an international examining committee of more than 30 medical and scientific specialists. Even if the experts fail to come up with a natural explanation, the church will throw out 50 percent of claims. Being adjudged a miracle is tough. Certainly there is a more critical analysis in place now than there ever was 2000 years ago!

The chapters of the book are thematic, and because so many of the miracle events selected also involve cures, there is no separate chapter for healing as there is in Part One.

Apparitions of Christ

Since Christ's ministry on earth, people have claimed experiences of his presence in a number of mysterious forms. Reports of visions and voices, of garments impressed with his features—even the "perfume of Christ"—have been investigated, testing scientists' resources to the limit.

In this chapter and the following one on the Apparitions of Mary, an apparition is defined as an image seen external to the body and mind, at a well-defined place, to which witnesses might testify. A private vision, therefore, even one as grand as that of Pope Leo XIII in 1884 about the 20th-century church, is an internal experience only and cannot count as a miracle.

These apparitions represent moments in a long line of divine revelation that emerges from time to time, rather like an underground stream occasionally meeting the surface. The content of such revelations does not always convey an immediate meaning. Sometimes they shock, and the church may deem it prudent to keep the message out of the public domain. Apocalyptic literature of the late Jewish and early Christian periods, likewise, delivered damning messages about the powers that be, often couched in terms that to us would seem like nonsense, but

which to their listeners,
who understood the
imagery, would reveal
divine intentions.

Unpalatable truths are
sometimes a feature of religious
experience. The Apocalypse of St. John
the Divine, in which Christ appears in the form
of a lamb bearing the marks of its slaughter, contrasts ironically the harmless
innocence of this creature with the force of its condemnation of the church. In
a similar vein, the messages of Christ entrusted to the Kenyan nun Anna Ali
condemn the sacrilegious behavior of some of today's priests. And the man
largely responsible for instituting Christianity, St. Paul, suffered the most
humbling experience of Christ before renouncing his former life.

St. Paul's Conversion

O ne of the most startling visions of Christ came to a Jew named Saul (Paul) bent on persecuting members of the new sect known as the Nazarenes, followers of Jesus of Nazareth.

[Acts 9]

Revelation or Crisis of Conscience?

——— ✳ ———

It has been suggested that Paul's conversion took place over a long period. Paul was one of the Jews involved in the stoning to death of Stephen, a Christian. As a result he may have suffered a reaction that culminated in a crisis of conscience on the Damascus road. The consequence of this was a psychosomatic illness— blindness—that passed only after he accepted the Christian faith.

Saul himself was a Pharisee, and was fanatical about strict observance of the Jewish Law. He regarded the Nazarene beliefs to be nothing less than blasphemy, and had sought permission from the High Priest to stamp out the cult by arresting any Nazarenes he might find and bringing them to trial. While he and his companions were on their way to Damascus (some 150 miles (240km) from Jerusalem), a light suddenly flashed from the sky. Falling to the ground in terror, he heard a voice addressing him, "Saul, Saul, why do you persecute me?"

Saul asked who this could be. The voice replied, "I am Jesus, whom you are persecuting. Get up and go into the city, and you will be told what you have to do." When Saul got up from the ground he found he could no longer see, and he had to be led by the hand into Damascus. He remained blind for three days, and during that time took no food or drink.

Left A representation from Gustave Dore of the drama of St. Paul's conversion on the road to Damascus.

Jesus also appeared to a disciple in Damascus called Ananias, telling him to go to the house of Judas where he would find Saul praying for the return of his sight. Ananias went and laid his hands on Saul, telling him that he had been sent by Jesus who had appeared to Saul on the road, and that Saul would be filled with the Holy Spirit. Immediately, scales seemed to fall from Saul's eyes, and his sight was restored. After being baptized, he used his other name, Paul, denoting his Roman citizenship, and was soon himself proclaiming the new faith publicly in the synagogues.

The holy Family of Bordeaux

[1822]

After the upheavals of the French Revolution of 1793–98, the church in France endeavored to make repairs, and several new religious institutions opened. One of them was a community of women called the Holy Family of Bordeaux, or Ladies of Loreto.

Father Delort, standing in for the regular priest of the institute, was to give the Benediction on Sunday, February 3, 1822. On arriving at the chapel, Fr Delort in the usual way uncovered the Blessed Sacrament and started blessing it with incense. However, before he had finished, something made him look at the monstrance (the gold vessel used to contain the wafers of bread). In place of the holy bread was an image of Christ—his head, chest, and arms. He was framed like a painting within the circular shape of the monstrance and, as the priest's testimony states, "the painting looked alive."

The figure, a beautiful man about 30 years old, was radiant white with a red sash draped over one shoulder and his chest. The head sometimes inclined from one side to the other, and the arms moved. Thinking it an illusion,

Left Radiant monstrance
from Florence, 1749.

the priest called over the altar boy who said he had already seen the miraculous sight, and could still see it. The priest threw himself on the floor and, as he looked upward, tears of joy welled in his eyes. The image of Christ remained throughout the service, which lasted about 20 minutes. Only when the priest came to place the monstrance back on the altar did the image disappear.

As soon as the priest left the chapel, the women attending the Benediction came up to him, said they had witnessed the miracle, and asked him what it could mean. The Mother Superior who was kneeling in the sacristy for the duration of the service also saw the image and, although she took it to be just an illusion, was so profoundly moved by the experience that she went straight home after the service without speaking to anyone. Only when people asked her about it did she realize that it was no illusion.

Pope Leo XII confirmed the miracle and instituted the feast of the Holy Family in commemoration of this event. *See also* Eucharistic Miracles, *page 90.*

Italy

Rome •

Mediterranean Sea

1987

Sister Anna Ali

More than a few eyebrows were raised at a press conference in Rome when a Kenyan nun not only related separate incidents when she claimed to have met Christ but also had the photographs to prove it.

Sister Anna Ali, whose father was a Muslim and her mother a Roman Catholic, was staying at the official residence of Archbishop Emmanuel Milingo in Rome in August of 1987 when the experiences started. Typically, they came before daylight, while she was at prayer. The room would fill with an azure light, and there, enveloped by the light, stood a man. She described him as having dark hair and wearing red. He delivered a series of messages about his anguish at the sins of his beloved priests, and the need of prayers for their atonement.

On the feast of Corpus Christi in 1988, Jesus apparently came to her in tears of blood, a phenomenon recorded in a photograph she took. She found that on the day before an apparition was due her face would swell up and become painful. The next day she, too, would weep tears of blood. On examination, her doctor found no medical explanation for the symptoms. What he did point out was an extraordinary aroma of freshness she exuded during the process, which has been described as "the perfume of Christ."

The Message of Christ

———✳———

In some revelations Jesus gave the reasons for his visitations. His words spoken through Anna Ali include the following: "Listen to me. I am above this earth. I make myself visible in order to bring back souls. I love mankind . . . Many do not listen to me because they do not believe in my reality. We should realize the infinite treasure in the Eucharist: As I am exposed I will pour infinite mercy in the hearts of souls."

But there is a warning: "Like a beggar, I ask for prayers and atonement . . . I suffer the pain of seeing souls fall into perdition. Satan has darkened the spirits which were already turbid. Evil turns against itself, like a horrible serpentine monster that unconsciously coils around souls. My warnings are not heeded! And the perverse world is like a persecuting dragon."

Rescue and Deliverance

People in peril tend to pray for help. Even seemingly impossible situations have sometimes been resolved by inexplicable happenings: A mist suddenly envelops a charging cavalry; an indestructible painting gives miraculous protection to its possessor; a nation is saved from starvation. Whether it is individuals or whole nations who are saved unaccountably, these are the types of miracle that mankind has always associated with a benevolent God.

Ever since the Red Sea parted to allow the fleeing Israelites an escape route to safety, there have been extraordinary reports of what is believed to have been divine rescue. The medieval theologian St. Thomas Aquinas formulated an extensive system of angelology in which he states that every soul has its guardian angel. Although angels, he maintains, cannot perform miracles, they can operate as God's instruments of miracles. When St. Peter escaped from prison, he was supposedly led away by an angel. When two British officers in the First World War faced almost certain death before a charging German cavalry, an "angelic mist" enveloped the enemy. Apparitions of Christ and Mary have also been reported at moments of release from perilous situations.

Sea of
Galilee

Jerusalem

Dead
Sea

St. Peter's Escape from Prison

[Acts 12]

When Agrippa I was king of Galilee and Judea (39–44 C.E.), he curried favor with his Jewish subjects by persecuting the hated Christians. First James, the leader of the Jerusalem church, was beheaded, then it was Peter's turn to face the music.

Guardian Angels

———— ✳ ————

Since the Middle Ages, the Catholic church has taught that everyone, good and bad alike, has a guardian angel. Angels offer protection and guidance, but their ultimate purpose is to help the soul achieve salvation. They are said to be attracted to the spiritually advanced and the innocent, and repelled by evil. Usually unseen, they influence us by "secret impulse," or intuition.

Peter was held in prison, under heavy guard. On the eve of his trial he was asleep in his cell, chained to two soldiers, while outside the door sentries kept watch. The cell suddenly filled with light and there stood an angel. Peter woke and found the chains loosened. The angel told him to gather up his things and follow him out. They passed the first guard post, then the second, and reached the iron gate leading out into the city. The gate opened of its own accord, and when they had walked the length of the street Peter found himself alone. He realized that he had been rescued from Agrippa.

When he arrived at the house of the mother of John Mark, all were praying for Peter's release. They could not believe that it was him and thought it must be his guardian angel.

Italy

Rome •

San Giovanni
Rotondo

Mediterranean Sea

The Conversion
of Emperor
Constantine

[312 CE]

A fter Constantine was proclaimed Roman Emperor in succession to his father Constantius in 306, he still had to overcome his rival, Maxentius, to secure the throne. The Battle of the Milvian Bridge in Rome delivered Constantine's enemy into his hands, but it also became the celebrated occasion of his miraculous conversion to Christianity.

What the Skeptics Say . . .

———— ✳ ————

The collapse of the Western Roman Empire prior to Constantine's accession left a power vacuum that was largely filled by the papacy. Constantine realized the route to power was through the church and set about gaining control of it. The claim to a divinely ordained conversion worked, for within a short space of time Constantine had collected much of the political power of the church into his own hands.

Alarmed by reports that Maxentius had mastery of magical arts and could employ them to his advantage in battle, Constantine sought divine aid to defeat his opponent and begged assistance from his father's monotheistic god.

The historian Eusebius of Caesarea, in whom Constantine confided, recounts: "While he was thus praying . . . a most incredible sign appeared to him from heaven . . . a cross of light in the heavens, above the sun, and an inscription, CONQUER BY THIS, attached to it. While he continued to ponder and reason on its meaning, night overtook him; then in his sleep the Christ of God appeared to him . . .

and commanded him to make a likeness of that sign, and to use it as a safeguard in all engagements with his enemies."

Thus Constantine put a cross on every one of his soldiers' shields before marching on Rome. He confronted Maxentius, who miraculously was induced to fight outside the city fortifications and was heavily defeated.

[1382]

The Black Madonna

T he embattled painting of Our Lady of Czestochowa, known as the "Black Madonna," repeatedly gave miraculous protection to communities under siege. It gained such a magical reputation that attackers were as intent on destroying the image as on capturing the enemy.

Cult of the Black Madonna

———— ✳ ————

Today, some 400 statues of Black Madonnas are known worldwide, with most in France. Usually situated in the quiet recesses of churches, they have black or dark faces and often stand on sites linked with pagan goddesses. Some consider the Black Madonna to be the iconic remains of prehistoric Mother-Earth worship.

According to tradition, St. Luke painted the portrait of Mary on a cypress table made by Joseph. Helena, mother of Emperor Constantine, discovered it in the fourth century and took it to Constantinople where it was housed in a chapel. When the city was under siege a fire destroyed the entire chapel except for the wall upon which hung the painting. The portrait's features were now blackened by soot.

In 1382, while the painting hung in the palace of Polish Prince Ladislaus, an invading Tartar pierced the throat of the Madonna with an arrow. Fearing for its safety, the prince took the portrait to a monastery on Jasna Gora (Mount of Light), near the town of Czestochowa. As the portrait's reputation grew, the monastery became a focus for Polish nationalism. When the Hussites overran it in 1430, the attempt to destroy the portrait failed. One of the marauders struck it twice with his sword before he fell

Left The Black Madonna: Our Lady of Czestochowa, Poland

to the floor writhing in agony and died. The sword cuts and the arrow wound have remained visible in the painting, defying all attempts to repair the damage.

In 1655, Poland was attacked by King Charles X of Sweden. The monks defended the portrait against a 40-day siege before the Swedes were eventually driven out of the country. After this rout the Lady of Czestochowa was officially named the symbol of Polish national unity and crowned Queen of Poland.

The Flying Monk

Italy
Rome •
San Giovanni Rotondo
Mediterranean Sea

[1943]

Allied pilots in the Second World War testified to seeing in the sky a flying monk whose outstretched arms repeatedly prevented bombs from falling on the town of San Giovanni Rotondo in Italy.

What the Witnesses Say . . .

———— ✳ ————

After the war the US commander went to the town to look for the famous priest with the stigmata named Padre Pio. As he entered the convent, he recognized a friar as that of the image in the sky. Padre Pio went to meet him and, putting a hand on his shoulders, said to him: "So it is you, the one who wished to do away with all of us." The general knelt down before him in awe. Later he converted to Catholicism.

In 1943, the Allies were launching air raids out of Bari, the US air base in southern Italy. Prior to Italy's surrender to the Allies, heavy bombardment of centers throughout Puglia were carried out. However, some reports were circulating that when missions flew in the vicinity of San Giovanni Rotondo, in the Gargano peninsula, pilots had the bizarre experience of seeing in the sky a friar with his arms raised above his head. Furthermore some sort of force emanating from him prevented their planes from flying into the airspace over the town. Despite the obliteration of the region, not one bomb hit the town.

San Giovanni Rotondo was a key target for the Allies, as military intelligence had discovered that a German arsenal of weapons existed there under guard. The operation was so important that the American commander decided to lead out a squadron of bombers himself. In due course he returned from the mission, apparently downcast. When curious pilots asked why, it transpired that he too had experienced the same mysterious phantasm, the same air resistance, and the inability of any pilot in his squadron to attack this seemingly "protected" town.

Left Try as they did, World War II bomber pilots were unable to hit their target.

Pacific Ocean

Manila •

Philippines

Soldiers at Manila

[1986]

A rigged election by President Marcos and popular unrest formed the troubled background to an extraordinary occurrence on the streets of the Philippine capital in February 1986.

What the Skeptics Say . . .

——✳——

There came a point when the soldiers realized their number was up. The crowd had swelled to such huge proportions, and the atmosphere become so intense, that to join ranks with the masses must have seemed the only sensible option.

Corazon Aquino was the people's choice to succeed Marcos and was considered without a doubt to have secured the majority of their votes in the election. However, through ballot-box stuffing and control of the media, Marcos declared himself the winner. Millions of Philippinos took to the streets in protest. One segment of the army attempted a coup but failed. Determined to keep political control, Marcos sent in a convoy of tanks manned by loyalist troops and the crack marine corps who swore absolute allegiance to their leader. Facing a huge crowd of demonstrating civilians, some of whom were lying down in front of the tanks, while others prayed with their rosaries, the tank personnel were given the signal to open fire.

At this point, according to Cardinal Sin who later spoke to many of the soldiers present, the marines who were riding on the top of the tanks saw in the clouds a bright image of the Cross, followed by the vision of a beautiful nun, dressed in blue, standing in front of the tanks. The nun then told them to stop what they were

Above Millions of people took to the streets to protest at the rigged election of President Marcos in the Philippines.

doing, and not to harm "her children." The soldiers were so overcome by the vision that they gave up the confrontation and climbed down from their tanks to join the people. Marcos was forced to flee the country.

Testimony of Sister Lucia

———✳———

The last surviving member of the trio of witnesses to the apparition of the Virgin Mary at Fatima was Sister Lucia. When Cardinal Sin of Manila visited her after the events described left, he discovered that despite living in a cloistered cell with no access to the media, Lucia knew everything that had happened in the revolution. Furthermore, she said Corazon Aquino was a gift from God and that her nation would help in bringing China to Christianity.

Apparitions of Mary

An ironic feature of Marian apparitions is that nearly always the figure is of a lovely, beautiful woman whose features suggest nothing but sweetness and light, yet the message she bears is one of stern admonition and warning.

Like those of Jesus, the apparitions are often experienced at times of stress—in war, persecution, and deprivation—and their purpose is to mediate God's displeasure at what humanity is doing. They carry messages urging people to prayer and righteous living, and warn of the consequences of continuing to follow sinful ways. Sometimes the warnings are presented in apocalyptic terms. As with the ancient prophets, the subjects selected for the mediumship of such revelations possess an unusual level of percipience. They can be religious or outwardly ordinary people, and

Church History of Mary

——— ✳ ———

1–4th c.	Church divided in beliefs.
5th c.	Officially declared "Mother of God"; widespread belief in her perpetual virginity.
6th c.	Belief in Assumption of Mary, body and soul, into heaven; first Marian haloes in art.
8th c.	Feast of Immaculate Conception first celebrated.
9th c.	Designated "Queen of Heaven."
1531	First Church-authenticated apparition.
1532–1830	No declared apparitions during Reformation and Inquisitions.
1854	Immaculate Conception becomes Roman Catholic dogma.
1950	Assumption of Mary becomes Roman Catholic dogma.
1950–2000	Increased number of apparitions with growing sense of millennial climax.

frequently children. Phenomena accompanying the apparitions can include visions of angels, heavenly music and singing, miraculous cures, luminosity, and divine messages.

Mary's role as intercessor on behalf of humanity, especially her devotees, has been a source of debate in the history of the church. Since the Reformation, Protestant churches have had difficulty in squaring the ideas of Mary as divine mediatrix with Christ as the unique mediator of salvation. Yet, as time moved ever closer to the end of the millennium, so the number of reported Marian apparitions increased, particularly after 1950, when the Assumption of Mary was declared a dogma of the Roman Catholic church. The church is guarded in its response to claims of apparitions. It often ignores or discredits them, and of those taken seriously, a painstaking and skeptical examination will be conducted before an apparition can be authenticated. While the Roman Catholic church teaches that God can grant private revelations by suspending natural laws and opening a window onto the supernatural world, its concern is whether their source is divine or diabolic.

Juan Diego of Guadalupe

T he first Marian apparition to be authenticated by the Roman Catholic church was witnessed by an Aztec peasant soon after the Spanish conquistadors had conquered Mexico.

[1531]

Gross maltreatment of the indigenous people, and the Spanish Bishop Zumárraga's decision to destroy all Aztec temples, pushed Mexico to the brink of insurrection. In the midst of this crisis in December of 1531, Zumárraga was visited by an Aztec convert, a peasant by the name of Juan Diego, who recounted his recent extraordinary experience. While walking to Mass he heard music coming from the top of a hill. He climbed to the summit and found there a beautiful lady who identified herself as the perfect and perpetual Virgin Mary and told him to build a temple at nearby Tepeyac, where she would heal all who suffered. She told him to report what he had seen to the bishop.

Zumárraga scoffed at the story and turned the peasant out. A further apparition failed again to convince the bishop who demanded a sign be sent from heaven as evidence. On his third visit to Tepeyac, Juan Diego saw beautiful flowers blooming impossibly in midwinter. Following instructions from Mary, Juan filled his tilma, a type of cape, and took the bouquet to Zumárraga.

Shocked though the bishop was to behold such a sight, it was as nothing compared to what followed. Impressed on the inside of Juan's tilma was a full-length image of the lady Juan had seen. As Zumárraga embraced him, word of the miracle spread. Soon thousands of Aztecs came to venerate the sacred image on the cloak which Juan placed in a chapel he built at Tepeyac. Within a matter of years, millions of Aztecs had embraced the Roman Catholic faith and the political crisis was at an end.

Above A depiction of Our Lady of Guadalupe with a background of midwinter scenery and unseasonal flowers in bloom.

What the Scientists Say . . .

———— ✳ ————

The tilma, made of ayate maguey cactus cloth, should have decomposed within 20 years, yet it still exists and shows no sign of deterioration. Most remarkable are the eyes in the image. Reflections in the pupils closely resemble those formed on the corneas of living eyes. Photographs of these reflections have been subjected to computer analysis and have been found to represent faces. Ophthalmologists are at a loss to explain the phenomenon. Is it possible that when Juan Diego unrolled the tilma in Zumárraga's office the facial expressions of those present were fixed for all time in the eyes of the image revealed?

France

• Lourdes

St. Bernadette of Lourdes

Scavenging for bones to make a stew was the unlikely start to a series of revelations that turned a cave in the French Pyrenees into the most famous healing shrine in the world.

[Matthew 1:18–2:2]

Examination of a Miracle Claim

———✳———

From many thousands of claims, the Roman Catholic church has officially recognized 65 miracle cures at Lourdes, the last one occurring in 1987. Before a "cure" is deemed to be a miracle, the case is examined by a medical bureau in Lourdes, then an international committee of 30 specialists. If a case passes these stages, it is regarded as extraordinary by science and medically inexplicable. It remains for the church to make a pronouncement.

One cold day in February 1858, Bernadette Soubirous and two companions were searching locally for food and fuel. Later the two girls found Bernadette kneeling at the entrance to a cave in a trancelike state. When her companions managed to shake her out of the trance, she told them she had seen a soft glow in the cave, and a beautiful lady appeared within the glow.

Three days later Bernadette had a similar experience. The village buzzed with excitement. There now began the so-called "fortnight of apparitions." Every day a huge crowd, which grew to several thousand, followed the seer to the cave hoping to witness a miracle. Eventually their patience was rewarded. After kneeling in prayer, and still in ecstasy, she began furiously digging at the earth. Muddy water welled up in the hollow she had made. She reported that a voice told her "to drink and wash at the spring and eat the green you find growing there." The crowd gasped as Bernadette emerged from "the grotto" (as it now became known) with her face covered in mud, chewing grass. The spring turned into a

Left An apparition of the Virgin Mary appearing to Bernadette Soubirous at Lourdes in 1858. Bernadette joined a convent where she remained for the rest of her short life, dying at the age of 35. In 1909, her body was exhumed and found to be incorrupt. She was canonized in 1933.

flowing stream, remarkably containing curative qualities. One man who had been blind in one eye could see again after bathing in the water. A woman who had suffered with paralyzed hands likewise regained their use. A further five miraculous cures happened at the spring that year.

News of the miracles spread like wildfire. The local priest became convinced when Bernadette reported the sixteenth apparition. The lady identified herself as the "Immaculate Conception" which he took to be divine confirmation of the Catholic dogma proclaimed by Pope Pius IX four years earlier.

Knock, Ireland

The church at Knock served just a dozen humble homes in an area blighted by the potato famine. Evictions of families too poor to pay the rent had left the hamlet in misery when, from nowhere, an extraordinary visitation changed its prospects.

[1879]

Witnesses

———— ✳ ————

This is the first Marian apparition to be witnessed by people other than the seer. Fourteen people gave testimonies. Some women tried to embrace the figures, but were unable to, finding no bodily substance. Despite rain, the ground beneath the figures remained dry.

Early in January 1880, apparitions were witnessed three more times by many people, including Archdeacon Cavanaugh, two policemen, and numerous pilgrims.

On a rainy day in August 1879, Margaret Beirne went to lock up the local church at Knock. As she turned to leave, she noticed a strange brightness covering the church. Independently, her sister Mary and the housekeeper of the church were walking along a road when they, too, noticed what one of them at first thought were new statues on the church. But as they got closer, they realized the figures were moving. Mary declared that it must be the Virgin Mary.

They and 13 others saw in mid-evening a beautiful woman, dressed in white garments, wearing a radiant crown. Her hands were raised as if in prayer. To her right stood Joseph with his head inclined toward her. On her left was thought to be St. John the Evangelist, dressed as a bishop, and to his left was an altar on which was placed a lamb and cross surmounted by angels.

The entire apparition appeared on the south wall of the church in a cloud of light and lasted for about two hours. Other villagers elsewhere

Above: Site of the apparition of the
Blessed Virgin Mary at Knock, Co. Mayo.

reported a strange bright light illuminating the
area where the church was situated.

There were subsequent reports of cures
associated with visits to the church. A 28-year-
old woman who had been deaf since childhood
regained her hearing on visiting the chapel.
Two blind men recovered their sight there. A
crippled woman was carried to the south gable
wall and then walked away without help.

What the Skeptics Say . . .

———— ✳ ————

Unusual "glowing balls"
of light were reported not
only at the church but also
in the vicinity generally.
Critics attribute this
phenomenon to "bog gas."

Atlantic
Ocean

Fatima
*

Lisbon *

Portugal

[1917]

Fatima, Portuga

T he events that took place at Fatima in Portugal are regarded as the greatest supernatural phenomena of the 20th century. Pope Pius XII said that the message of Fatima is one of the greatest interventions of God through Mary since the death of the Apostles.

In a hilly area near the town of Fatima, three peasant girls had a vision of a woman who called herself "Our Lady of the Rosary," otherwise known as the Blessed Virgin Mary. The first appearance was on May 13. Five more visitations occurred, each time on the 13th day of the month.

Mary told the children she had been sent by God to deliver a message. Coming at a time of great violence in the First World War, she explained that the war was a punishment for sin, and that heaven would only grant peace to the world if her requests for prayer and reconciliation were obeyed.

The core of the message is contained in what is called the "Secret." It consists of three parts. The first part was a horrifying vision of hell. The second prophesied the outbreak of the Second World War, and as a condition of world peace requested the return of Russia to the Roman Catholic faith. The third part has not yet been made public, but was written down by one of the three seers, Lucy Dos Santos, and is held in the Vatican.

Dance of the Sun

As a culmination of the visions, Mary promised that God would work a great miracle in October "so that all may believe." The event was reported in newspapers around the world, and by October 13, 1917 more than 70,000 people had gathered in the Cova da Iria, near Fatima, to witness the miracle.

On the sixth and final day of visitation, Lucy saw the Blessed Virgin point to the sun. She excitedly repeated the gesture and the crowd looked into the sky.

The rain stopped, the clouds parted, and the sun shone, not with its usual brilliance but like a silver disk, pale as the moon. The disk began to whirl in the sky and cast off shafts of multicolored light across the sky in all directions.

After a few moments, the wonder stopped, but resumed again a second and a third time, with the sun spinning at even greater speeds. Then a gasp of terror rose from the crowd as the sun seemed to come crashing down to earth. Just as the terrified people thought they would be destroyed the miracle ceased, and the sun resumed its normal place in the sky, shining peacefully.

Left Vision of the Virgin Mary at Fatima, May 13, 1917. On the same day in 1981, Pope John Paul II was saved from an assassin's bullet by turning to look at a girl wearing a picture of the Virgin Mary.

• Garabandal

Spain

[1961]

Garabandal, Spain, 1961

San Sebastian de Garabandal is a small village located in northwest Spain. On June 18, 1961, four girls, all aged 11 or 12, were playing on the outskirts of the village when there appeared before them a radiant vision, resembling a young boy, with reddish translucent wings.

After a series of appearances, the angel announced that there would be a manifestation of "Our Lady of Mount Carmel" the following day. At about 6 p.m. on July 2, as a horde of villagers, reporters, and priests followed the seers to the place of the apparitions, an image of the Virgin Mary appeared with two angels. Hovering above the Virgin was an extraordinary image that the girls described as "the eye of God."

Each time that the girls experienced an apparition they would fall into rapture. Their heads were thrown back, their pupils dilated, and their faces were imbued with "an angelic countenance." The girls would walk at high speed, arm in arm, looking skyward yet having no difficulty in crossing the rocky terrain. Stranger still, sometimes the girls would fall backward, stiff as boards, without injuring themselves, and then rise to their feet again without apparently needing to use their limbs.

What the Scientists Say . . .

———— ✳ ————

Doctors and psychiatrists rigorously examined the visionaries while in ecstasy. Not one of a whole range of tests including pinpricks, burns, and spotlights shone into the girls' eyes, produced any reaction. A pediatrician certified that the girls were normal and that the ecstasies could not be classified under any known physiological phenomenon.

[Matthew 1:18–2:2]

Mama Rosa o
San Damiano

Suffering from advanced intestinal tumors and peritonitis, 52-year-old Rosa Quattrini was discharged from the hospital in Italy with little hope of a cure. Then a visit one day from a stranger changed her life.

As she was lying in bed in great pain, Mama Rosa, as she was known locally, received a visit from an unknown lady who said she had been sent by Padre Pio, a friar famous for his clairvoyance. The day was September 29, 1961, the feast day of the Annunciation to Mary. When the Angelus bell rang out from the village church, the two women said the usual devotional prayer. Afterward the lady asked Rosa to get up from her bed, and she placed her hands on the affected area. Immediately, the pain ceased. Doctors later confirmed that the tumors and the peritonitis had disappeared.

Mama Rosa visited Padre Pio in the village of San Giovanni Rotondo where she was told to dedicate herself to relieving the sick at Piacenza hospital where she had been a patient. She was also told that a special mission awaited her. On October 16, 1964, again while reciting the Angelus, Mama Rosa heard a voice outside. In the garden, suspended above a pear tree, was an apparition of the Virgin Mary. Rosa was told

The Spinning Sun

———— ✳ ————

As in Fatima in 1917, extraordinary solar phenomena were observed on December 9, 1968. The Piacenza daily newspaper reported that 10,000 people gathered in the rain at San Damiano to witness the sun apparently moving in unnatural courses, including spinning and coming to rest on an illuminated cross. An image of a monk, thought to be Padre Pio, was also seen suspended in the sky. Hundreds of photographs of the phenomena were examined in Paris at the National Office for Study and Research in Air and Space, but no explanation could be offered. Skeptics claimed the photos were either fake, or represented unknown atmospheric phenomena.

to dig a well beside the tree. To prove Mary's appearance the tree would bloom, Mama Rosa was told, even though blossoms usually only came in the spring. The next day everyone gathered, and in astonishment beheld the tree full of fragrant blossoms. From the well, curative water sprang, and the blind, deaf, and paralyzed were healed. Several more apparitions to Mama Rosa followed.

Accompanying the manifestations of Mary were messages expressing sorrow at the lack of faith in the world, and the possibility of a coming apocalypse. *See also* The Flying Monk, *page 66, and* Fatima, Portugal, *page 78.*

[1968–70]

Zeitun, Egypt

In a suburb of Cairo, a Coptic minority clustered around the Church of St. Mary, built on the site where traditionally the Holy Family settled after escaping King Herod's attempts to destroy the newborn Messiah. It was above the dome of this edifice that more than a quarter of a million people witnessed the luminous figure of the Virgin Mary at the end of the 1960s.

What the Skeptics Say . . .

———※———

During the term of President Nasser, which ended in 1970, the Soviets were influential in Egyptian politics and were reckoned to be projecting the image of the Virgin Mary using Telstar space-satellite technology. However, even if this were feasible, it is not understood why anti-religious Communists should wish to bolster the faith of Christians around the world.

On April 2, 1968, two car mechanics happened to glance at the church and were amazed to see a "nun" dressed in white standing on top of the dome. Thinking she was going to jump, one of the men ran for help while the other called a priest. A crowd gathered and shouted to the "nun" not to jump, but gradually the image of her faded and eventually vanished. Seven days later the figure returned, and continued to fade and reappear at intervals until 1970.

Most of those present could see the image well. The figure floated around the roof of the church, descending to the edge of the roof's pitch. One witness, a priest who saw the apparition several times, said it was usually heralded by brilliant flashes of light, like sheet lightning, about a quarter of an hour beforehand. Sometimes mysterious clouds, rare

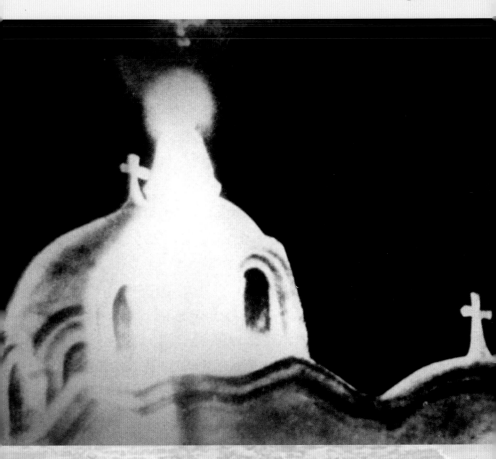

in Cairo, would form around the church like a canopy. Luminous birdlike shapes appeared for an instant, gliding around the apparition before disappearing. Witnesses described the phenomenon as beautiful. Mary herself would bow, greet, and bless the gathered people, who would fall to their knees simultaneously.

The Coptic religious weekly *Watani* published regular updates of the events, which included miraculous cures among the pilgrims present. Some of the confirmed cases included the healing of urinary bladder cancer, cancer of the thyroid gland, blindness, deafness, limb paralysis, and a number of viral infections.

Above Vision of the Virgin Mary, on the roof of the Coptic Orthodox Church of St Mary, Zeitun, Egypt, 1968.

Kibeho, Rwanda

Rwanda

Kibeho •

A hot and desolate land, barely able to support the villagers of Kibeho, was the unpromising source of an extraordinary series of wonders for the people of Rwanda.

[1981]

Apocalypse Foretold

——— ✳ ———

As well as trances, some of the seers fell into comas that lasted two to three days. While comatose, the children experienced "tours of horror." In August 1982, five of the seers reported the same vision of torrents of blood, unburied bodies, decapitated heads, and trees on fire. Mary warned them to leave Rwanda.

Years later, the genocidal wars between the Hutus and Tutsis raged out of control and the prophecies were fulfilled.

In this most unfruitful of dustbowls there appeared to eight children the image of a woman, robed in a sparkling white veil. Falling into ecstatic trances, the visionaries would lose contact with the world for a while and behold wondrous green meadows filled with flowers and glittering with dew. Overhead, in a sky they described as soft and pink, floated the Virgin Mary, smiling down upon the craned heads of her young seers.

The first apparitions took place in the dormitory of a school. As interest grew, space was made by moving the seers to the courtyard outside. The Virgin always announced the date of her next appearance, so masses of pilgrims had time to gather, including many priests and nuns. Thousands saw how a spectrum of colored light passed through the sky over Kibeho, and how the stars at night turned into luminous crosses. The Virgin's messages would be repeated by the seers through a loudspeaker system so that all could benefit from the revelations. Familiar themes of admonitions for lack of piety and belief in the "things of heaven" were delivered. Then, unusually, the Virgin asked a question of one of the seers, Anathalie: "Why have you not asked me for water? I will now give you a rain of consecration."

It was August, a time when it seldom rained. Shortly afterward the first of many downpours fell over the land. No one ran for shelter. Instead, the gathered pilgrims knelt down in the mud and praised heaven. Containers were put out to collect the rainwater, which was even found to have curative qualities. A spontaneous renewal of faith spread through the country promising a brighter future—yet this outpouring of goodwill proved to be short-lived.

Bosnia
Herzegovina

· Medjugorje

Medjugorje, Bosnia

Within a Croat enclave of the former Yugoslavia, now Bosnia, were reported a number of mysterious sightings reminiscent of those witnessed at Fatima in 1917.

[1981]

What the Government did . . .

———— ✳ ————

Fearing a resurgence of Croat nationalism, the Communist government prohibited access to the area. A priest who took charge of the seers was imprisoned and tortured, but his jailers are reported to have backed off after they saw rays of light in his cell. The church is investigating the claims of the Medjugorje miracle.

One midsummer evening in 1981, three girls and a boy were walking on the slopes of the Crnica mountains to the south of the village of Medjugorje. Suddenly they saw a light on the hillside, and within the light a young woman holding a child. At first, the children fled, but curiosity got the better of them and the next day they returned with two others—this time the apparition smiled. The whole village buzzed with excitement, and in two days a crowd of 2000–3000 from the surrounding villages gathered. No adults could see the apparition, though everyone saw miraculous lights at the foot of the hill.

The seers had conversations with the apparition who gave messages of warning. Identifying herself as the Virgin Mary, she announced that a period of darkness had enveloped the planet and that the world must seek peace and be reconciled. Over the next 18 months, Mary appeared every day to at least one of the six children, and by 1985 nearly 2000 visitations had occurred.

In August 1981, other mysterious phenomena were witnessed by some 150 onlookers. In a cloudless sky, the sun became a white disk and emitted multicolored rays. It was seen spinning, expanding, and contracting until a white cloud settled on the hill of the apparitions. The Croat word for peace, Mir, was emblazoned in light above Mount Krizevac, across the valley, for all to see. As if these solar phenomena were not sensational enough, a huge stone cross erected on the mountain was seen to spin around, and in the sky above it angels accompanied a woman standing against a luminous globe.

Eucharistic Miracles

At the heart of both Roman Catholic and Eastern Orthodox belief lies the idea that Christ physically comes into us through the rite of Holy Communion, the swallowing of the bread and wine, which is believed to have become the body and blood of Christ. It is not surprising that down the centuries many of the devout, particularly the saints, have had mystical experiences associated with the Eucharist, yet records even give details of miraculous transformations.

Hosts (consecrated bread) have "bled" at the altar. They have changed into human flesh. Eucharistic wine has turned into blood. Hosts have levitated into the air, and have been preserved for centuries. There are accounts of saints receiving Holy Communion from Christ himself, such as St. Clement, 4th-century bishop of Ancara. St. Catherine of Siena experienced ecstasies after receiving the Eucharist from Christ and angels, and claimed to be able to distinguish between consecrated and unconsecrated bread. Saints have spent nights in rapture before the Eucharist without the least sign of fatigue the next morning. Some have been so imbued with holy grace as to experience bodily levitation.

Numerous though the accounts of these eucharistic miracles are, Roman Catholics believe they are simply manifestations of the ultimate miracle recorded in the New Testament, "the Word became flesh, and dwelt among us." (John 1:14) As the incarnation of God on earth, Jesus promised a continuation of his presence among the faithful. At the Last Supper he foretold that he would give

his flesh and blood as food and drink: "Take, eat. This is my body . . . Drink ye all of this. For this is my blood." These words have been accepted in their literal sense as a Roman Catholic article of faith, known as the Real Presence of Christ, ever since the 13th century. It is understood that the priest's act of consecration at the altar changes the entire substance of the bread and wine, so that only their appearances—color, taste, smell—remain.

Reports of eucharistic phenomena have peppered church history ever since c.250 C.E., when St. Cyprian noted flames issuing forth from the tabernacle in which the Eucharist was kept. However, never have so many eucharistic miracles been witnessed over such a short period as they have been in the final decade of the last millennium.

Lanciano, Italy

Italy
Lanciano
Rome
Mediterranean Sea

[8th Century]

A priest of the Order of St. Basil was struggling with his faith, in particular the belief that the eucharistic bread and wine transformed into the actual body and blood of Christ. While he was celebrating Mass one day at the Church of St. Longinus, the Italian priest was to have his faith reaffirmed in a startling manner.

What the Scientists Say . . .

———※———

In 1970, fragments of both the "flesh" and the "blood" underwent laboratory analysis. The flesh was found to be tissue from the heart wall. The pellets were found to be human blood. The blood showed no signs of decay. On the contrary, its protein ratio suggested that it was fresh. The findings concluded that a fraud perpetrated centuries ago was impossible.

He had just uttered the words of consecration at the altar when suddenly around the host appeared a circle of flesh, and the wine visibly changed into blood. When he had recovered from the shock, he turned to the congregation and invited them to come up and see it for themselves. Word spread, and it was not long before the whole town had been to see the eucharistic miracle.

As time went by, the flesh remained intact but the blood in the chalice divided into five pellets of different shapes and sizes. Strangely, on weighing the different pellets on a pair of scales, the monk found that any one pellet was equal in weight to any or all of the others put together. The host and the pellets of blood were kept in an ivory reliquary until 1713, when they were transferred into a richly ornamented monstrance, thought by some to

Left The circle of flesh that appeared miraculously around the eucharistic wafer (now decayed away) was examined in 1971 and found to be muscular tissue of the human heart. No preservative agents were found.

be the original one in which the miraculous change occurred. The occurrence at Lanciano was the first recorded eucharistic miracle of the Real Presence of Christ.

Rome

Italy

Copertino

Mediterranean Sea

[1603–63]

St. Joseph of Copertino

According to records, many holy persons have experienced the sensation of being lifted into the air without physical assistance, a phenomenon known as levitation. The saint who is credited with more levitation than any other is Joseph of Copertino in southern Italy.

Levitation

————— ❋ —————

St. Teresa of Avila levitated before witnesses during mystical rapture. She said, "It seemed to me as if a great force beneath my feet lifted me up."

Levitation is not confined to the Christian tradition. Islam, Hinduism, and Buddhism all record instances. In 1936, an Indian yogi, Subbayah Pullavar, levitated in front of 150 people. He lay horizontal in a trance 3 feet (1m) off the ground for about 4 minutes.

Born in a stable to a poor woman whose husband had died during the pregnancy, Joseph had a tough early life. He was mocked at school for being stupid and having a gaping mouth. Despite little education, Joseph was accepted to take orders for the priesthood at a local Franciscan monastery, and it was then that his life began to change. Although he could only just read, his learning surpassed that of the other friars. He underwent severe ascetic practices, and acquired a reputation for his devotion. He led an increasingly mystical life.

One year, on the day before Good Friday, Joseph was praying. Bowed silently in supplication, his fellow monks became aware that he was rising from the floor. The genuflecting figure moved toward the vessel containing the Eucharist and remained suspended in the air, rapt in

Left Joseph of Copertino, or the "Flying Friar," as he was nicknamed, so disturbed his superiors that he was banned from celebrating Mass publicly for 35 years.

adoration of the holy sacrifice of Christ due to be celebrated. Only when his superior called him did Joseph return to the place where he had begun praying.

On more than 70 occasions, Joseph levitated. A number of dignitaries testified to his "holy flights," including the philosopher Leibnitz and the Spanish ambassador to the Pope. As Joseph sat dying, his doctor noted that he floated 6 inches (15cm) above the chair and murmured that he could hear and smell paradise.

[1962]

Garabandal, Spain 1962

The year after miraculous events had begun to overtake the remote mountain village of Garabandal, a further sensation was to surround the young seer Conchita. A great gasp of anticipation followed the announcement of a date in the near future when this "little miracle" would bless the community.

What the Church Says . . .

———※———

The bishops at Santander refused to admit the divine origin of the events at Garabandal. At the time, a church decree was in force forbidding any unauthorized Catholic involvement in miraculous events. In 1966, Conchita was called to Rome and interviewed by Pope Paul VI who gave her his blessing. Later that year the decree of prohibition was rescinded.

The whole of Spain tried to squeeze into Garabandal in time for July 19. The sheer volume of cars and buses brought the entire district to a standstill. Pilgrims came armed with cameras and tape-recorders, ready to catch the supernatural event. On previous occasions, the young female seers had stuck out their tongues in a state of religious ecstasy, later explaining that they were receiving Holy Communion from an angel. The host, though, was always invisible.

As nightfall came, the crowd grew more and more excited at the prospect of a miracle unfolding before its eyes. It was not until the early hours of the morning that Conchita left her house in the familiar trancelike state and proceeded to the famous spot among the pines where the earlier Marian apparitions had occurred. The girl suddenly fell to her knees and stuck out her tongue. Those near enough confirmed that her mouth was empty. Then, quicker than the eye could see, there suddenly materialized on her tongue a brilliant white host, delivered according to Conchita by the Archangel Michael as promised a fortnight earlier. The host remained visible for some two minutes, and was captured on film as a small orb of glowing light by an amateur cameraman.

Below Conchita is receiving invisible but real Communion from St. Michael.

Worcester, Massachusett

[1996]

A n ordinary residential street in Worcester, Massachusetts, provides the home of a teenage girl proclaimed as a living saint. Her popularity is such that bookings to visit her have to be taken 18 months in advance. The person that will be seen is bedridden and unable to move or speak, a condition she has suffered since a swimming-pool accident left her paralyzed at the age of three.

What the Skeptics Say . . .

———※———

All the claims associated with Audrey Santo—oozing oil, blood, stigmata—could be hoaxes. Skeptics say that the Santo family is trying to compensate for the loss of their daughter's health and find payment for medical bills by selling videos and samples of "holy" oil.

Since 1987, Audrey Santo has taken sustenance via a pipe to her stomach. The only food admitted orally is Holy Communion, which she takes daily. To help with the procedure, the local bishop allowed the Sacrament to be kept in a tabernacle in Audrey's room. On Good Friday 1996, one of the nurses who takes care of Audrey noticed that the tabernacle had begun dripping a reddish fluid. When the host was taken from the tabernacle, it was also found to be "bleeding". On examination in a laboratory, the fluid was said to be human blood. Audrey herself now manifests the stigmata, the visible wounds of Jesus' crucifixion.

Two engraved angels on the tabernacle door sometimes weep scented oil. Mysteriously, chemists have not been able to verify the constitution of the oil.

—————✳—————

There are some non-theological explanations for eucharistic bread turning a reddish color, of which the most common is the presence of the bacterium *serratia marcescens*, which grows readily on starchy food, and looks like a blood-red coloration to the ordinary eye. Under a microscope, however, it appears quite different, and can be distinguished easily from human blood.

The Stigmata of Christ

The ultimate embodiment of the sacrifice of Christ—in all its painful, gruesome aspects—is the bearing of the wounds, or stigmata, of Christ. Ever since St. Francis of Assisi first manifested them in the 13th century, more than 300 individuals have been recorded in the history of the Christian church as suffering such extraordinary phenomena.

In every case, religious ecstasy and an identification with Christ's Passion appear to trigger the onset of the stigmata, which, in their fullest extent, include the wounds resulting from nails driven through the hands and feet, a lance in the side, a crown of thorns wreathing the head, and scourging across the back and shoulders. Often at first the stigmatic suffers the pain invisibly and later develops the visible wounds. They may appear and disappear without obvious cause, and in many cases they recur when the stigmatic is undergoing an intense period of religious devotion. The degree of affliction varies from the weeping of blood through the skin, to actual puncture wounds. Sometimes protuberances of the flesh resembling nails have formed on the hands and feet. Although the wounds may remain open for long periods, there has been no known instance of infection or disease, nor on the other hand of any natural healing process.

The stigmata follow no common pattern of appearance, and will often reflect the placement of crucifixion wounds found on the personal object of a stigmatic's contemplation. This suggests to skeptics that the process of stigmatization is entirely the result of the workings of the mind and has no foundation in a supernatural world. It is noteworthy that cases are known of Muslim stigmatics bearing wounds that correspond to those received by Muhammad in battle.

The view of the Roman Catholic church is ambivalent. While the phenomenon is not considered to be a reliable sign of personal sanctity, theologians generally agree that the stigmata, which is rare, occurs only as a result of religious ecstasy, which in turn is deemed to come from God. The usual scriptural point of reference is St. Paul's Letter to the Galatians, 6:17, "I bear on my body the marks of Jesus," though it is not known whether this declaration refers to wounds resulting from persecution, or from the stigmata.

La Verna·
Rome·

Italy

Mediterranean Sea

[1224]

St. Francis of Assisi

The medieval Italian friar who founded the Order of Franciscans was the first person to have the sacred stigmata, the body marks corresponding to the wounds of the crucified Christ. After a life of passionate devotion to God and man, St. Francis began to manifest this miraculous phenomenon while on a mountain retreat.

Eyewitness Report

———※———

Preserved in Assisi is an account of the miracle written by Brother Leo who was with St. Francis at the time. In the wounds of the feet and hands were outgrowths of flesh representing nails—on one end they had round black heads; on the other, long points which bent back and grasped the skin. The saint's right side is described as bearing an open wound as if caused by a lance.

Early in August 1224, Francis retired with three companions to La Verna in the Apennine Mountains of central Italy to keep a 40-day fast in preparation for Michaelmas. Close to the climax of the fast, the Feast of the Exaltation of the Cross (September 14), Francis saw a vision of an angel. Immediately afterward there appeared on his body the visible marks of the five wounds of Christ. Marks appeared on his hands, feet, and near the heart (corresponding to the lance wound), also on the head (crown of thorns), and on his shoulders and back (carrying of the cross and scourging).

The stigmata caused great pain and further weakened a body already worn out by years of austerity. He was ordered to see doctors, but none of their treatments helped. He died aged about 45, two years after receiving the wounds.

Right
St. Francis
receiving the
stigmata on
Mount Verna.
His wounds were
witnessed by his
brethren and
contemporary historians.

What the Scientists Say . . .

———— ✳ ————

Some physiologists have said that the wounds might be produced by the action of autosuggestion, or the imagination, coupled with lively emotions. Being renowned for his devotion to Christ, St. Francis' meditation on Christ's suffering on the cross would have intensified through the 40-day period of fasting. It is suggested that his preoccupation with this acted on him physically, reproducing the wounds.

While no one claims that the imagination will produce wounds in a person who is in a normal state of mind, the question is more difficult with persons who are in an abnormal state, such as ecstasy or hypnosis. Hypnotism has, in rare cases, induced colored sweat, a poor imitation of the symptoms of stigmata. The only means of proving scientifically that the imagination may produce stigmata is by producing manifestations of it in the natural order. This has not yet been achieved.

Italy

Rome

San Giovanni
Rotondo

Mediterranean Sea

[1887-1968]

Padre Pio

Baptized as Francis, Padre Pio joined the Capuchin friars at the age of 15. Before becoming a priest, he heard a voice prophesying that he would be "scourged and nailed to the Cross."

On September 20, 1918, the prophecy was fulfilled. He described the experience in a letter he wrote a month later to his spiritual advisor:

"In the choir, after I had celebrated Mass, I yielded to a drowsiness similar to a sweet sleep. All the internal and external senses and even the very faculties of my soul were immersed in indescribable stillness.

"While this was taking place, I saw before me a mysterious person . . . his hands and feet and side were dripping blood. The sight terrified me and what I felt at that moment is indescribable . . . The vision disappeared and I became aware that my hands, feet, and side were dripping blood. Imagine the agony I experienced and continue to experience almost every day. The heart wound bleeds continually, especially from Thursday evening until Saturday."

From then on the stigmata did not stop weeping blood for some 50 years, until a few days before he died when they disappeared. Doctors estimated that he lost blood amounting to about a teacupful every day.

Bilocation

———✷———

Some holy persons have been credited with the facility of appearing in two distant places at once. It is thought that the individual projects a double, which is perceived by others as a solid physical form or as a ghost. Many saints and mystics have been famous for bilocation. Scientific evidence is inconclusive, and skeptics believe the phenomenon is produced by a mental exercise in an altered state of consciousness.

News of this wonder spread throughout the world, and scientists came to make their assessments. No natural explanation could be offered.

The wounds caused Padre Pio great pain, which he suffered gladly as "the flames of divine love." To take Mass, which was attended by large numbers, he wore white gloves to hide what he considered to be embarrassing. As he took Communion, he would fall into religious ecstasy and his whole body would shake with the pain.

He was blessed with other divine gifts, such as bilocation, prophecy, the "perfume" of Christ, reading of souls, and the ability to heal others. People are still being cured through his intercession.

See also The Flying Monk, *page 66*; Mama Rosa, *page 82*.

Left Padre Pio with the wounds of the stigmata, which he suffered for 50 years.

Berlin
Germany

• Konnersreuth

Therese Neumann

A mystical nun from Bavaria is believed to have bled every Friday from the wounds in her hands and feet, and on Good Fridays suffered the agonizing pain of Christ's crucifixion.

[1898–1962]

What the Scholars Say . . .

————— ✳ —————

In his book *The Bleeding Mind*, Ian Wilson argues that the bleeding is self-induced by individuals who are undergoing extreme personal stress. He says that sufferers turn to prayer to escape the torments of the self. It is the mind, he believes, that produces the stigmata, even such nail-like protuberances from the flesh as St. Francis of Assisi suffered.

Before she developed the stigmata, Therese Neumann from Konnersreuth experienced two mystical connections in her twenties. Years of illness had kept her blind and bedridden. On the day that Teresa of Lisieux was beatified in 1923, Therese regained her sight, and then two years later was able to walk again, on the day Teresa was canonized. In March 1926, wounds appeared on the back of each hand and on the instep of each foot, with no known cause of injury. From then onward, for more than 30 years, the wounds would open every Friday, and each time Therese would lose up to a pint of blood. On Good Fridays she bled from her hands, feet, side, head, and shoulder, even her eyes, as she experienced the passion and death of Christ in religious ecstasy.

During this long period of bizarre existence, Therese is said to have eaten nothing but the Communion wafer and wine. Doctors state that her excreta ceased after 1930, and her intestinal tract shriveled.

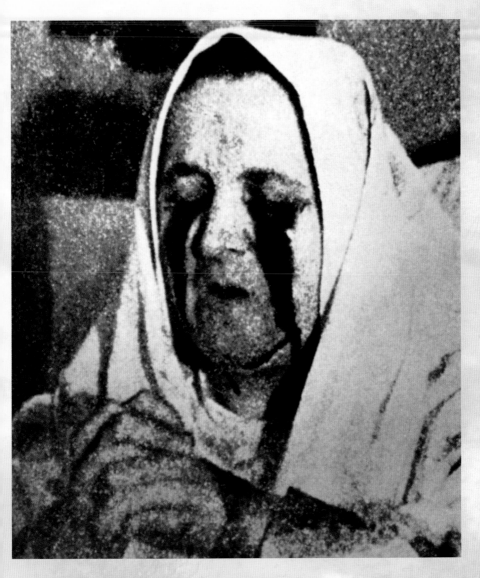

Nevertheless, she remained active until her death at the age of 64. Her hometown of Konnersreuth is now a center of pilgrimage.

Above Therese Neumann during her passion ecstasy on Good Friday.

U.S.A.

Lake Ridge

[1991]

James Bruse, Virginia, USA

A Roman Catholic priest made the news headlines when he developed the stigmata on his wrists and feet. His presence also appeared to coincide with the weeping of icons.

Variation in the Wounds

———— ✳ ————

The wounds of the stigmata do not appear the same in all who have suffered them. One stigmatic, for example, showed only those caused by the crown of thorns; two others had only the lance wound in their side. Most stigmatics have wounds in their palms, yet James Bruse suffered the stigmata in his wrists. This variation may relate to the different methods of crucifixion.

Thousands of visitors came to St. Elizabeth Ann Seton Church in Lake Ridge, Virginia, hoping to see the reported miracles associated with the gentle assistant pastor who started developing the five wounds of Christ in December. His superior in the parish witnessed the markings and also noticed a statue in his room bleeding. He said that naturally he doubted the phenomena at first, but could not otherwise explain what he plainly could see. A *Washington Post* reporter also witnessed the phenomena, including, on another occasion, the tears being wept by a statue of the Madonna in a church where James Bruse conducted Mass. A sense of divine presence seemed to follow him around and pervaded any space he occupied. Those present said they could smell the sweet fragrance of roses when there were none in the church.

Churchgoers have taken photos of the weeping statues, and one said that a statue wept while he was holding it in his hands. The phenomena continued well into 1993.

Right The Gospels say Jesus was nailed through his palms; the more usual Roman method was to nail through the wrists.

Weeping Statues

Among the most impressive and widespread phenomena of the last decade of the 20th century were weeping Christian statues. Of particular interest are statues of the Virgin Mary that originated from shrines, such as Medjugorje in Bosnia, where she is reputed to have appeared.

Just as Medjugorje is linked thematically with earlier apparitions at Garabandal and Fatima, it is thought that a spiritual thread of revelation is continuing through these weeping icons. The message of suffering, and the call to prayer and reconciliation that is common to these revelations, is believed to be symbolized in the tears shed by Mary and Jesus at the end of the millennium.

The Roman Catholic church, which worries that people may concentrate more on supernatural occurrences than on a life of faith, has adopted a typically guarded stance. Investigations into miracle claims take longer than has so far been available for pronouncements to be made on any of the events detailed in this chapter. The ones selected are those that are most promising. Only one weeping Madonna has been officially authenticated, a statue of the Virgin Mary at Siracusa in Sicily in 1954. Sightings are often reported at times of social and political tension. Nevertheless, it has to be said that, with some miracle claims, the scientific evidence is so strong that even diehard skeptics are scratching their heads for an explanation.

The phenomenal rise in recorded instances of weeping icons in the 1990s produced more than its fair share of fraudulent cases. In 1994, an organization was set up in Italy to expose religious and occult fraud and extortion. Of the 5000 cases examined, 200 were followed up by the police investigating fake healing and fortune-telling.

San Thomas
Mexico
Pacific Ocean

[1992]

San Tomás, Mexico

A 12-year-old girl drew thousands of pilgrims to a remote Mexican village after her prayer for a miracle was not only answered spontaneously but also accompanied by visible signs associated with supernatural intervention.

Ana Avila visited a local shrine of the Virgin Mary and prayed for her mother who was dying of cancer. As she knelt before a 3-foot (1m) statue of the Madonna, she looked up and saw tear droplets rolling down the cheeks of the statue. Thinking it must be morning dew, the girl touched the droplets and tasted them. It was strangely salty, just as a real tear would be. When she returned home, she was amazed to find her mother, who had been confined to her bed for months, walking about the house, apparently cured of her disease.

The good news spread through the village and beyond, and into the national newspapers. Other cures were also reported in connection with the same statue. The local priest, Father Amoros, says people have come from many parts of the world to see the miraculous Madonna. People, he says, had arrived on stretchers and crutches, and walked away free of infirmity after they had prayed before the statue and touched its tears.

What the Scientists Say . . .

———— ✳ ————

Several scientists from Mexico City and the USA have carried out their examinations. All say the tears are real, but none can offer an explanation of where they come from or how they heal the sick.

Right A Madonna's tears are said to express the sorrow felt by the Virgin Mary at the suffering and injustice in the world.

Italy

Civitavecchia

·Rome

Civitavecchia, Italy

A statue of the Virgin Mary, brought from the Marian shrine of Medjugorje in Bosnia, became the mysterious fount of "tears of pain" when it was set up as a garden shrine near Rome. Furthermore, the lacrimation was not of the usual salty water kind, but of blood.

[1995]

What the Labs Reveal . . .

———✳———

Analysis showed the blood to be human and male. One professor suggested carrying the investigation further by comparing the DNA of the supposed tears of blood with that of the male members of the Gregori family. The church sees the gender identity as significant in symbolizing the blood of Jesus, which is shed through his mother to indicate the depth of pain he is suffering over the state of the world.

Fabio Gregori had asked a priest who was going to Medjugorje to bring back a replica of the Virgin Mary so that he could construct a stone grotto in his garden for Our Lady. On February 2, the Feast of the Presentation of Jesus in the Temple, his five-year-old daughter Jessica went into the garden and shouted to her father that Mary was crying. Her father saw for himself tears of blood that streamed down the cheeks, leaving behind red traces.

Fabio went to the church and described what had happened. The priest and others who attended Mass hurried to witness the weeping statue. Soon thousands of visitors were filling the street to catch a glimpse of the miracle. Police authorities complained to the local bishop, who was dismayed at such superstitious hysteria. He took the statue to his home.

Nothing more remarkable happened until March 15, when the same bishop, Monsignor Grillo Girolamo, received a visit from two nuns who asked to venerate the statue. The bishop knelt with

Left Tears of blood on the Rosa Mystica Statue of the Virgin Mary. Her emblematic rose signifies the "odor of sanctity," which smells identical to the scent of roses and is emitted by some statues of the Madonna.

his guests in prayer. Just as he took the statue in his hands, he saw red liquid welling from its eyes. The bishop described how spiritually uplifting the experience had been. The lacrimation was the fourteenth and last one of this statue to occur at Civitavecchia, which is now a place of national pilgrimage and devotion.

Muna.

Spain

Mura, Spain

Yet another statue brought from the Marian shrine of Medjugorje has become the focus of miraculous phenomena. Just as in the village of Civitavecchia in Italy three years earlier, a marble statue of the Madonna has produced tears of blood in its new setting.

[1998]

The 22-inch (70-cm) high statue was placed on a tall pedestal in the village square at Mura, north of Barcelona. On the morning of March 16, 1998, Father Lluis Costa was clearing up some flowers when he noticed what looked like bloodstains on the face of the statue. Father Costa noted that there was no sign that the statue had been moved as the dust around it had not been disturbed.

He noticed two blood nodules on the eyelids of the Madonna whose eyes were half-closed. Expert advice confirmed that the spread and coagulation of blood from these nodules to the corners of the eyes and down the cheeks conformed to the natural course that tears would follow. Doctors also confirmed that the blood could not have been injected into the marble as it would have coagulated inside.

Father Costa believed it to be a message from God. He said, "When a mother cries, it is a bad thing. And if the tears are of blood, it means the pain is deep. These miracles are like a warning, a cry without words, to which people are free to listen or not."

Relics

If weeping statues became the miracle craze at the end of the second millennium, the relics of saints and all things to do with Jesus hit the spot with fervent believers in the Middle Ages. Believing is always easier if there are things to see and touch. The precious bones and blood of Christian martyrs were displayed in cathedral shrines throughout Europe to help the devotion of worshipers who believed that the holy articles were invested with supernatural powers capable of effecting miraculous cures.

Traditions enhancing the importance of relics abounded in the Middle Ages. Crucifixion relics included the crown of thorns, the spear of the Roman Longinus, the holy reed, and the holy sponge, and all reached the West sometime in the Middle Ages. Indeed, the trafficking of religious articles was so great that it was said that enough wood had derived from the "fragments of the Cross" to build a ship!

Perhaps the most celebrated relic is the Turin Shroud, venerated as the winding sheet of Jesus' burial, and still the subject of debate among scientists and historians regarding its authenticity. Also contentious is the Veil of Veronica. It is said that when Jesus reached the sixth Station of the Cross in the Via Dolorosa, a lady of Jerusalem by the name of Veronica wiped his face with a handkerchief. His divine countenance was thus imprinted on the cloth, which became one of the most venerated relics in the Roman Catholic church.

Relics assumed such great charisma in the minds of ordinary folk that many went to enormous lengths to see them. Although the Catholic church today would say that relics should be regarded only as aids to faith, and not objects of faith, it was not slow to foster the popular belief in the Middle Ages. Pilgrimages to such centers as Santiago di Compostela in Spain and Walsingham in England were common. What is more, countless testimonies of miraculous cures of "the deaf, the blind, the wounded, the leprous, and the tempest-tossed" circulated.

And who are we to say that the devotees of these relic shrines were not "miraculously" healed of their ailments? The whole phenomenon of the "power to cure" seems to reside so much within the scope of individuals that there is no denying the possibility exists that mere "aids to faith" can be invested with life-transforming properties.

The Turin Shroud

T he most famous and controversial relic of Christendom is the burial cloth in which Joseph of Arimathea purportedly wrapped the crucified Jesus. Imprinted on the fabric is the image of a tall bearded man of distinguished countenance with Middle Eastern features. For centuries the shroud's authenticity has been debated, but despite tests from a raft of modern scientific applications a unanimous verdict has proved elusive.

The evidence is compelling. The linen cloth is consistent in its fiber content and type of herringbone weave with that used in Palestine in Jesus' time. Pollen grains of several plants known to have existed in Jerusalem, but not in Europe, were detected in the fiber, as were mineral particles similar to the limestone of Jerusalem. When the church reluctantly allowed the shroud to be photographed in 1898, all were amazed to see a picture with much more detail than could be seen with the naked eye. It was as if the photo had been developed from a negative. People speculated that the image on the cloth had been formed at a moment of flashing light, which some believed was produced at the moment of Jesus' resurrection from the tomb.

The "messianic" shroud came to Turin

What the Scientists Say . . .

———— ✳ ————

The shroud was submitted for radiocarbon dating tests. Fragments were sent to Arizona, Oxford, and Zurich for independent assessments. In 1988 all three centers stated that the cloth was made from flax cut between 1260 and 1390, and was therefore a medieval forgery.

However, these results have been contested: the cloth was damaged by two fires in its history, which may have altered its carbon composition, making it seem younger.

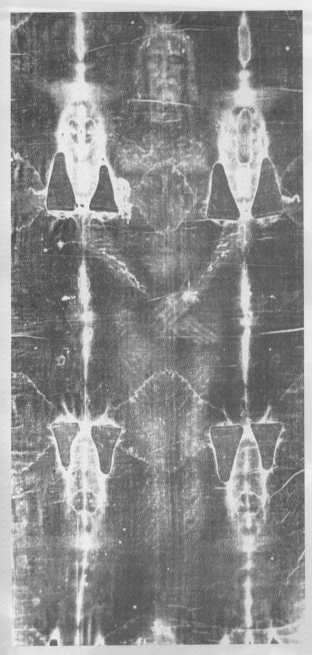

Left The manner of the shroud's creation remains a mystery. Computerized enhancement has ruled out the idea that the image was painted onto the cloth.

from France in 1578. Nothing is known of it before the 1350s, when it was owned by a French knight and denounced as a fake by the local bishop who said he knew the artist who made it. Some say there was no earlier history. Tradition says the cloth was taken from the empty tomb by one of Jesus' disciples, Thaddaeus, and brought to Edessa, now Urfa in Turkey. A shroud bearing the image of Christ, called the Mandylion, was discovered there in the 6th century and moved to Constantinople. When Crusaders sacked the city in 1204, it disappeared and is thought to have been taken to France. The question is whether the Mandylion is to be identified with the shroud that turned up in France and was later enshrined in Turin.

Micropedia of
Modern Miracles

Stich, Germany 1970, A Bleeding Eucharist

In a tiny hamlet in Bavaria on June 9 and again on July 14 red stains, approximately the size of the host, appeared on the altar corporal (the white linen cloth on which the Eucharist is placed) after the consecration. The chalice had no leak, and no drop of eucharistic wine was spilt. The cloth was photographed and dispatched for chemical analysis. The results showed that the stain was caused by human blood containing biochemical markers of a man in agony. On the second occurrence an image of the cross was seen on the stain.

Bayside, New York City 1970, A Seer

Thousands prayed with Veronica Leuken, a seer of the Virgin Mary who had revealed herself as the Lady of the Roses. Numerous photos taken of Veronica during prayer vigils show beams of light shining down on her from above. Another Polaroid shot shows an image of the Virgin Mary above a church in Bayside. Messages delivered include predictions of ecological disasters, the emergence of mysterious diseases, a war causing the destruction of cities, and earthquakes in New York, as well as the startling assertion that Pope Paul VI would be replaced by an impostor in 1975.

London, 1970s
Healing

Property consultant Maurice Tester suffered from a prolapsed disk that doctors said could be cured only by operating, and then with limited hope of success. He went to see a healer, Ted Fricker, who treated him by lightly running his hand up and down the patient's back. In ten minutes, the pain he had suffered ceased, and after a few more visits he was cured. His specialist confirmed total cure and said natural remission was impossible. Fricker says his power to heal comes from God, and that he simply follows directions given to him by inner voices.

Akita, Japan 1973,
Apparition and Stigmata

Sister Agnes Sasagawa was deaf when she experienced light flooding out from an open tabernacle of the Eucharist. The Virgin Mary appeared to her and healed her affliction, though it was replaced by the stigmata (wounds of Christ). Among the messages Sister Agnes received daily was one delivered on October 13 that warned of a chastisement with fire falling from heaven that will wipe out most of humanity, and of the devil's infiltration into the church. A statue of the Virgin Mary at Sister Agnes' convent has shed tears on more than 100 occasions.

Betania, Venezuela 1976,
1984, Apparition of Mary

On March 25, 1976, as predicted, the Virgin Mary appeared for the first time in Betania, announcing herself as Mary Virgin and Mother Reconciler of People and Nations. She continued to appear to individuals, but in 1984 she was witnessed clearly by 150 people. The diverse group included children, students, and medical and professional people.

Walsingham, England
1988, Solar Phenomena

On August 4, at one of Europe's greatest medieval shrines, there were reports of solar phenomena. Constantly changing colors—blue, green, yellow, red, and purple—formed circles that emanated from the sun toward the viewers. The sun appeared like a white eucharistic wafer, and seemed to spin toward earth and then return to its position in the sky. Five or six smaller suns revolved around the sun,

which turned red. The estimated 500 observers, who were mostly Roman Catholic, all thought they were witnessing a miracle.

Knoxville, USA 1995, Cross of Light

Pilgrims and skeptics have witnessed a 40-foot (12-m) cross of light at the Copper Ridge Baptist chapel in Tennessee. The minister of the chapel, the reverend Joe Bullard, and his wife were the first to see the mysterious phenomenon. Since then its fame has grown. On January 5, 1996 the fiery cross was broadcast in a news bulletin on CBS-TV, when the church appeared to be on fire with the cross of light shining through each of its five windows.

Toronto, Canada 1996, Weeping Madonna

In a Greek Orthodox church in Toronto a painting of the Madonna was shedding tears. A replica of the 8th-century icon began weeping after Sunday Mass, leaving a puddle on the floor. The Reverend Katseas says the icon has the power to heal, and he believes the phenomenon to be a prophecy, which may be good or bad. The tears were preserved in a bottle and found to be fragrant.

Bethlehem, Israel 1996 Weeping Icon of Christ

A Muslim woman who had been coming to clean the Bethlehem Church of the Nativity for 22 years saw a light issuing from a picture of Jesus that hangs above the traditional birthplace. Then she saw one of his eyes wink, and red tears stream down his cheeks. Numerous Christians of different denominations, Jews and Muslims all testify to the phenomenon, as does a skeptical, lapsed Catholic journalist.

Cameroon 1998, Christ Encounter

Edwige Mbalikoung, 24, from Abong Mbang, was suffering in the hospital from a severe undiagnosed disease. She claims to have received visits in her dreams from Christ who told her to go home, pray, and read the Psalms. When she obeyed, an insect came out of her head. Her father burnt the insect and she was healed. While she was telling her story to skeptical listeners, Jesus appeared again. This time the stigmata appeared in her hands, as though providing proof to the skeptics. Edwige says her stigmata have the power to heal.

Index

Credits

Quarto would like to thank and acknowledge the following for supplying pictures reproduced in this book:

AKG, Berlin: 15, 35, 55, 67; Art Directors & Trip Photo Library: 83; Ann Ronan Picture Library: 33, 39, 43, 45, 53, 63; Ann Ronan, Musee de Conde, Chantilly: 19; Ann Ronan, V & A Museum: 23; Edimedia/Tate: 47; Fortean Picture Library: 13, 65, 73, 75, 77, 79, 85, 87, 97, 105, 107, 111, 113, 115; Fortean Picture Library, Dr. Elmar R. Gruber: 27, 103, 121; Frati Minori Conventuali, Lanciano (Chieti), Italy: 93; Gamma, Paris: 69; Penny Cobb: 86–87 background; Santuario San Guiseppe da Copertino: 95.

All other photographs and illustrations are the copyright of Quarto. While every effort has been made to credit contributors, we apologize should there have been any omissions or errors.